Visions and Healing
in the Acts of the Apostles

How the Early Believers
Experienced God

John J. Pilch

LITURGICAL PRESS
Collegeville, Minnesota

www.litpress.org

1	2	3	4	5	6	7	8

Library of Congress Cataloging-in-Publication Data

Pilch, John J.
    Visions and healing in the Acts of the Apostles : how the early believers experienced God / John J. Pilch.
        p. cm.
    Includes bibliographical references.
    ISBN 0-8146-2797-8 (pbk. : alk. paper)
    1. Bible. N.T. Acts--Commentaries.   2. Visions in the Bible.
3. Healing in the Bible. I. Title.

BS2625.6.V57P55   2004
266.6'07—dc22   2004001513

Dedicated with love and gratitude to
Dr. Felicitas Daniels Goodman,
respected anthropologist,
mentor and friend,
whose life and research have charted the way
to alternate reality, the realm of God.

Contents

Introduction

> "When he [Jesus] had said this, as they [the Apostles] were looking on, he was lifted up, and a cloud took him from their sight" (Acts 1:9).

> "But he [Stephen], filled with the holy Spirit, looked up intently to heaven and saw the glory of God and Jesus standing at the right hand of God, and he said, 'Behold, I see the heavens opened and the Son of man standing at the right hand of God'" (Acts 7:55-56).

> "On his journey, as he was nearing Damascus, a light from the sky suddenly flashed around him. He fell to the ground and heard a voice saying to him, 'Saul, Saul, why are you persecuting me?'" (Acts 9:3-4).

> "He [Peter] was hungry and wished to eat, and while they were making preparations he fell into a trance'" (Acts 10:10).

> "Cornelius replied, 'Four days ago at this hour, three o'clock in the afternoon, I was at prayer in my house when suddenly a man in dazzling robes stood before me. . . .'" (Acts 10:30).

These are just five of the more than twenty references in Acts of the Apostles to individuals encountering God, the risen Jesus, or angels in a level of awareness different from ordinary waking consciousness. Cognitive neuroscientists and anthropologists call these different levels of awareness altered states of consciousness (ASC). In general, they agree that at all times and in all places people have been capable of and actually entered a variety of altered states of consciousness. "Indeed the potential to shift, voluntarily or involuntarily between different states of consciousness is a function of the universal human nervous system. All people have to cope with different states of consciousness in one way or another" (Clottes and Lewis-Williams 1996: 12).

Even those in Western culture who because of their scientific and psychological socialization tend to be skeptical about or even resistant to these experiences have more of them than they realize. Those who drink alcohol know the effect of one, two, or more drinks on consciousness. Those who drive automobiles admit that they have often arrived at their destination having observed all the laws and followed the correct roads but can't remember the trip. The driver, especially if driving alone, has been in an altered state of consciousness commonly called "road trance." Practically everyone has daydreamed in class, or during a lecture, or a sermon, or a concert, or on many other occasions. These are all instances of altered states of consciousness, changed levels of awareness. As the examples just mentioned suggest, levels of awareness change often during a day: preparing a meal, listening to a lecture, driving, watching TV, and so on. Most of the time a person is unaware of the shift and realizes it only when forced to return to that from which he or she was "distracted." Moreover, scientists know precious little about the relationship among the more than twenty different levels of awareness identified (Goodman 1973: 101).

The reason why this experience is so universal is because it is rooted in the basic physiological make-up of every human being (Pilch 2002c). All human beings are 100% the same, 100% different, and 50% the same and 50% different all at the same time. At the level of biology, all human beings are 100% the same (barring handicaps or the like). The nervous system functions the same in all human beings no matter where they live or in what century. Of course, the country, culture, society, and family in which they live make them partly the same as other human beings and partly different, that is, 50% the same and 50% different. Every human being has a father and mother, but those roles are interpreted and experienced differently in different countries, cultures, societies, and families.

Some cultures (like ancient Israel) are patriarchal, others (like the Philippines) are matrilineal. The role of father and mother differs in each.

Relative to the topic of this book, Mediterranean believers are more likely to interpret an altered state of consciousness experience as an encounter with someone from the realm of God, while a scientifically sophisticated Western believer may be inclined to interpret such an experience as a "hallucination," that is, something pathological, or perhaps an "alien from outer space" or an "unidentified flying object (UFO)." The society, country, or culture of origin influences the way in which the visionary interprets an experience. In their ecstatic trance experience of Jesus' Transfiguration (Luke 9:28-36), the disciples identified the two men talking with him as Moses and Elijah, not Zeus and Apollo. Finally, as distinct individuals, every person is 100% different from any and every other person. The experiences of one person are not the experiences of another.

Dr. Erika Bourguignon was the pioneer in doing research on altered states of consciousness. Her work was further developed by one of her students, Dr. Felicitas Goodman. Dr. Goodman began her graduate work at a later time in her life after a successful career in linguistics. She was quite understandably drawn to research glossolalia, or "speaking in tongues," found in some religious groups. Her published research on that topic is one of the definitive studies of this phenomenon (Goodman 1972). Her interest in religious experience continued to grow, and in 1979 Dr. Goodman established The Cuyamungue Institute in Columbus, Ohio, and Santa Fe, New Mexico, an anthropological research and teaching institution specializing in comparative religions and ecstatic trance. In her long years of research and practice she examined artifacts and studied ethnographies to assist her in interpreting strategies for inducing changes in levels of awareness. She was and continues to be interested in the cross cultural phenomenon of altered states of consciousness identified as religious ecstatic trance. She also immersed herself in the study of mythologies to help her interpret many personal trance experiences which initially she could only remember and record. Often it was much later that she found the key to interpreting the experience. Interpretation of the experience is crucial, for the meaning of the experience is not always self-evident (see 1 Cor 14:13).

Based on her field work and research into religious ecstatic trance experiences, Dr. Goodman identified four major kinds of ASCs that serve four human needs or desires (Goodman 1990: 71-75; Gore 1995): (1) healing, that is, the restoration of meaning to life (e.g., Acts 3:4); (2) divination, that is, seeking or learning the answer to a question or solution to a problem (e.g., Acts 16:9-10); (3) metamorphosis, the blurring of the boundaries between the human world and the realm of God in hopes of learning how to work change that is needed and/or desired (e.g., Acts 12:6-11); (4) and sky (or spirit) journeys, that is, visits to the realm of God similar to those reported by the astral prophets Ezekiel (e.g., Ezek 3:23-24) and John in Revelation (e.g., Rev 4:1-2). As is evident in the scripture citations noted in the parentheses of the previous sentence, the trance experiences reported in Acts fit into Dr. Goodman's categories. (Though not reported in Acts, Paul admits in 2 Cor 12:1-5 that he experienced a trip or sky journey to the realm of God.)

In her early research, Dr. Goodman concluded that "the trance experience itself is vacuous. If no belief system is proffered, it will remain vacuous. It is a neurophysiological event that receives content only from signals present in the respective culture" (Goodman 1990: 17). However, Goodman's subsequent research proved that neurophysiological events are not really vacuous, but always occur in the context of a belief system, a mythology, an ideology. Her research confirmed that statement (Goodman 2001: 9). Trance experiences are thus filled with culturally significant and expected scenarios. Without a key to interpret the experience, the visionary believes it to be vacuous. But with the aid of a belief system, the visionary can interpret the visuals and provide the sound track and the interpretation. The understanding and interpretation of a vision derives from the culture, more specifically from what anthropologists call culture's latent discourse, or traditions of the culture, or "cultural dogma" (Goodman 1973: 101). A person learns and remembers these traditions, relying upon them for making sense out of experiences as needed.

In our scientific minded culture, the latent discourse responds with skepticism to any mention of altered states of consciousness experiences. Indeed, ASCs are often considered to be pathological or signs of pathology. In our culture, people who hear voices and communicate with persons who aren't there are said to be mentally ill. In contrast, in the biblical world the latent discourse is basically the Israelite tradition that believed that God's communication with human beings in altered states of consciousness was normal. "During the time young Samuel was minister to the LORD under Eli, a revelation of the LORD was uncommon [literally: "rare"] and [ecstatic] vision infrequent" (1 Sam 3:1). The Prophets of Israel as well as members of the Jesus movement and subsequent Jesus groups all shared a common latent discourse. They interpreted their trance experiences within a framework that ASC experiences were normal. The dramatic change and reinterpretation of God's rules about clean and unclean foods (see Leviticus 11) that Peter learned in his trance reported in Acts 10 could only happen in an ASC experience of beings from the realm of God communicating to a human being. Only God could make that change, and in the Israelite tradition just cited God routinely communicates with human beings in trance experiences.

The experiences, research, and publications of Dr. Goodman and her associates in The Cuyamungue Institute provide very helpful models and insights for analyzing and interpreting the reports of religious ecstatic trance experiences in Acts of the Apostles (Goodman 1990: 59). In this book I apply those insights to those reports in Acts of the Apostles. I follow a modified outline and the literary interpretation of Acts presented by

F. Scott Spencer (1997, see Appendix 1). Because he utilized and incorporated in his excellent literary analysis the cultural research of members of The Context Group of which I am a founding member, my approach complements his work.

It is also appropriate to review the basic, commonly held scholarly opinion about Acts. This commentary accepts that opinion, in general. While Luke claims to have made a careful investigation and an orderly presentation of his findings (Luke 1:1-4; compare Acts 1:1-2), scholars agree that he has interpreted events heavily. "In our view, the Lukan picture of Paul represents a literary fiction, and for the estimation of the social position of the historical Paul, his own letters have priority. The historical Paul was a citizen of neither Rome nor Tarsus" (Stegemann and Stegemann 1999: 302). Indeed, in a forthcoming commentary on Paul's letters, Prof. Bruce Malina and I argue that Paul was an Apostle to the lost sheep of the house of Israel living among the non-Israelites and not an Apostle to non-Israelites as presented by Luke in Acts (Malina and Pilch 2006). Yet even Luke indicates that Paul always insisted on his authentic and unquestioned status as an Israelite who was always open to dialogue with other Israelites. In the course of this commentary on Acts, I will indicate where Luke does not present Paul in his proper historical setting.

This raises a significant question about the double focus of this book: trance experiences (visions) and healing reports. Did these occur factually, or are they simply Lucan literary creations to make a "theological" point, or a mixture of fact and interpretation? As Prickett (1996: 45) observes, this question is inappropriate for a document like Acts of the Apostles.

> Yet in secular literature, chronicle and even in history, the boundaries between "fact" and "fiction" were not those that a modern audience would necessarily take for granted. The Latin word *historia* covered both "history" and "story" in our modern sense. The Elizabethan chronicles were by no means simply factual accounts of events—raw material, as it were, awaiting the shaping hand of the true historian. They were in many

ways as midrashic as the books of the Old Testament. It is no accident that, for instance, Stow's Chronicles of England (1580) repeat the story, first related by Joseph of Exeter and Geoffrey of Monmouth, of the foundation of Britain by Brutus, great-grandson of Aeneas. His capital on the Thames, Troynovant (or New Troy) later became London, and among his descendants were Gorboduc, Cymbeline, Coel (Cole: the 'merry old soul' of nursery rhymes) and Arthur.

Once we start to think of the problems and questions behind apparently self-evident notions like "history," we can see how relatively modern too is our seemingly straightforward distinction between "fact" and "fiction"—which does not date back much beyond the end of the eighteenth century and the work of such historians as Niebuhr and von Ranke. It is worth remembering that the origin of the word "fact" lies not in any notion of objectivity but in the Latin factum: "a thing done or performed."

Thus, to apply the notions of fact or fiction to Acts would be anachronistic. The more appropriate question would be "how should a contemporary reader imagine Luke's reports of visions and healings in Acts of the Apostles?" Whether a reader chooses to interpret some reports as factual (e.g., Paul's surviving the bite of the snake—Acts 28:5-6), or as core fact with [heavy] interpretation (e.g., Paul's call by God in a trance experience—Acts 9:1-9, compare with Gal 1:15-16), or as literary creation with historical elements interjected (e.g., Acts 27, the adventurous sea journey into which Paul and some of his visions have been inserted), the ultimate question concerns the cultural plausibility of the report. How would Luke's audience hear and interpret these reports?

At the conclusion of this commentary, I present a ceremonial rite for inducing trance (see Appendix 3). This rite was developed on the basis of insights from the research of Dr. Goodman and my familiarity with and experience in the Christian tradition, especially the Franciscan School. St. Bonaventure is recognized by the Church as the Prince of Mystical Theologians, and St. Joseph of Cupertino was so well known for his trance journeys and levitations that he was designated the patron of aviators.

The Bible in general and Acts in particular nowhere present the reader with a complete report containing all the elements and/or stages of a trance experience as they are known today from anthropology and cognitive neuroscience. The Bible is a high context document, that is, its authors assumed the original audience would be able to supply details that are not explicitly mentioned. To facilitate the reading of this commentary, therefore, I will summarize at this point the more detailed information about rite and trance presented in Appendix 2, and the elements and stages of trance presented in Appendix 3.

Trance experiences which are one of the many levels of awareness available to human beings can be spontaneous or induced. Daydreaming and reverie are examples of spontaneous trance. These changes of awareness occur frequently throughout the course of a day. In Acts of the Apostles, I identified fourteen examples of spontaneous trance: an angel gives instructions to Philip (Acts 8:26-40), Ananias learns about Paul's experience on the road (Acts 9:10-16); Agabus predicts a famine (Acts 11:28), etc. (see Appendix 3).

Intentionally induced trance ordinarily occurs in the context of a rite. Rites are structured, repetitive, and rhythmic patterns of behavior (see Appendix 2). This behavior has sometimes been called "ritual," but from a social science perspective that word is inappropriate as will become clear in a moment. There are two kinds of rites: a ritual rite, a behavior that occurs irregularly in day to day life, and a ceremonial rite, a behavior that occurs with regularity. Healing takes place in a ritual rite, that is, a behavior that is enacted only when someone is sick and seeks healing. Peter "stares" at the lame man and heals him (Acts 3:4; "staring" is often part of the ritual rite of healing). Paul "stares" at the blind man and heals him (Acts 14:8-10). Staring induces trance, and healing often takes place in trance (e.g., both of these deeds by Peter and Paul just mentioned).

Ceremonial rites occur with regularity in human life at predictable times and moments. Fixed prayer is one example of a ceremonial rite. Paul was at prayer in the Temple when he was advised in trance by the Lord to flee Jerusalem (Acts 22:17-23). The report of Paul's experience is brief. How is a reader to imagine the rite by which Paul entered a trance state and received instruction from the Lord? I summarize here the model which I have constructed and presented in Appendix 3. This model incorporates insights from cognitive neuroscience and anthropology.

1. Sensory deprivation (e.g., fasting)	Peter was hungry and at prayer on the rooftop when he saw the sheet with "unclean" foods (Acts 10:10)
2. An appropriate place	Paul was at prayer in the Temple when the Lord advised him to flee Jerusalem (Acts 22:17-23)
3. Technique for inducing the trance (a posture; scripture reading; prayer; meditation; etc.)	Peter was at prayer when his vision occurred (Acts 10:9-23)
4. Preparing oneself/one's body (purification rite: incense, prayer, etc.)	Cornelius was at prayer when the angel visited him (Acts 10:3-6)
5. Preparing the mind (a "concentration" exercise such as breathing, etc.)	No "exercise" is mentioned, but a number of experiences took place in the context of prayer.
6a. A trance neurologically stimulated from the "bottom up" (overstimulating the senses)	Paul "stares" at the lame man and heals him (Acts 14:8-10)
6b. A trance neurologically stimulated from the "top down" (in the brain)	Pondering the meaning of his first vision (Acts 10:10-16), Peter receives further instruction from the Spirit in trance (Acts 10:19)
7. Recording and interpreting the trance experience	The speeches of Peter interpret trance experiences (Acts 2:14-41, etc) as Paul interprets his call vision three times (Acts 9; 22; 26)

There are also three stages to the actual trance experience apparently reflected in Luke's report of Paul's call vision (Acts 9; 22; 26). These stages and their characteristics describe the neurological changes in a person experiencing altered states of consciousness and are documented by modern scientific technology.

Stage 1	the visionary sees geometric patterns; light (white) color
Stage 2	the visionary imposes meaning on these patterns
Stage 3	deepest stage; the visionary enters into the scenes and becomes part of the imagery

The reader will recognize that no report in Acts of the Apostles (or elsewhere in the Bible) reflects all the elements in this model. As anthropologists are careful to point out, a model tries to be comprehensive, to include everything the researcher has learned in many cultures. Yet every element may not be reported, indeed might not even have occurred in a given experience. The model is therefore heuristic, that is, it aids in understanding and interpretation. It is not prescriptive, that is, it does not say that every human experience must be like this.

Though I am aware that my research is making a scholarly contribution to the interpretation of Acts of the Apostles, I have written this book for pastoral purposes. At the recommendation of my Context Group Colleagues, especially Stuart Love, Dennis Duling, S. Scott Bartchy, and Bruce Malina, I changed my initial plan of focusing only on trance experiences and healing in favor of presenting the reader with the broader context of these events in Luke's total storyline spanning nearly forty years (A.D. 30±–A.D. 65±). For this purpose, I have relied heavily on F. Scott Spencer's presentation of the storyline as noted above. To enhance the pastoral utility of this book, I have prepared reflection questions for the reader in personal or group study. I owe a special debt of gratitude to Mrs. Loretta Fitzgerald Bedner, chairperson, department of religion, Bishop McGuiness Catholic High School, Kernersville, N.C., for assisting with these reflection questions.

Finally, in addition to Dr. Goodman whom I lovingly acknowledged in the dedication, I wish to thank Judy Lazarus and Joan Scott, members and officers of The Cuyamungue Institute and facilitators of the group that meets weekly in Davidsonville, Md., for initiating me into the research procedures of the Institute and for their continuing wise guidance along the way. With their assistance, I have a earned certification from the Institute to assist in research projects about religious ecstatic trance. Many of the insights gained from that experience and research have helped to illumine Luke's reports.

Feast of St. Joseph   John J. Pilch
of Cupertino, O.F.M. Cap.   Georgetown University,
September 18, 2003   Washington, D.C.,
University of Pretoria, South Africa,
and Studium Biblicum Franciscanum,
Hong Kong, SAR, China

Chapter 1

Acts 1–2
The Journey Begins

Communal Religious Trance Experience (ASCs)

ACTS 1:1-26 ASCENSION

In the opening verse of Acts of the Apostles (1:1), Luke connects this work with the gospel by referring to that book first and then repeating the name of the recipient, Theophilus, very likely the patron who supported the evangelist in the writing of these two volumes. The first two chapters of Acts report three "group" style trance experiences: Jesus' ascension into the sky (Acts 1:6-11); the group's reception of the holy Spirit (Acts 2:1-4); and a larger group experience of glossolalia (Acts 2:5-13; though some scholars consider this to be xenoglossy, an impression that Luke intentionally creates, glossolalia is a more plausible view, which I will explain below). The entire chapter one of Acts forms a literary unit about the ascension of Jesus bounded by an *inclusio* in v. 2: "the day he was taken up" and v. 22: "the day on which he was taken up from us." (An *inclusio* or inclusion is a literary device by which an author signals his intention that the verses included between these should be considered as a unit. The device is also used in musical composition and in film.)

Acts 1:1-11   Group trance experience of the risen Jesus' ascension

In the final chapter of his Gospel, Luke reported four things: the women's discovery that Jesus' tomb was empty (Luke 24:1-12), the risen Jesus' journey and discussion with two disciples on the road to Emmaus (Luke 24:13-35), an appearance of Jesus to the disciples in Jerusalem (24:36-49), and his ascension to the sky (24:50-51). All the events apparently took place in one day, the day Jesus was raised from the dead. At the beginning of his companion volume to the Gospel, Luke reports that Jesus "presented himself alive to them [his Apostles] by many proofs after he had suffered, appearing to them during forty days. . ." (Acts 1:3). Luke is the only one in the New Testament to mention this forty-day period, but scholars agree that it is best not to take the number literally. Not only is forty a symbolic number in the Bible, but added to Passover week it approaches the fifty days between the beginning of Passover and the beginning of Pentecost.

The sacred authors agree that after his crucifixion and burial, Jesus was seen "alive" (see Luke 24:5, 23; Acts 1:3) by different people on more than one occasion. These people truly saw the risen Jesus in altered states of consciousness experiences. These people, then, are "witnesses" of his being raised from the dead. In addition to the Apostles (see Acts 1:8, 22; 2:32; 3:15; 5:32; 10:39-41; 13:31), these witnesses include Paul (Acts 22:15; 26:16) and Stephen (Acts 22:20) and many others unnamed (1 Cor 15:6). Witnesses require a time of preparation to carry out their function (see Acts 13:31), and forty days in the Bible is a time that symbolizes adequate preparation to fulfill an appointed task (Exod 24:18; 34:28; 1 Kgs 19:8; Num 13:25; 14:34; Mark 1:12-13; Matt 4:1-11; Luke 4:1-13). This lengthy preparation period indicates that these witnesses testify to more than what we might call a "factual event." They must also proclaim its significance.

While a change in levels of consciousness takes place in an individual person, sometimes a group can share in that experience. Thus, the risen Jesus appeared to Mary Magdalene alone (John 20:11-18). Yet the Gospels also report that the risen Jesus appeared to groups of apostles (Luke 24:13-35; 36-39). Paul notes that Jesus appeared "to more than five hundred brothers at once" (1 Cor 15:6). Anthropological research indicates that while trance is indeed the experience of an individual, a group experience appears to enhance the potency of the trance. Each person adds support and intensity to the group's visions (Gore 1995: 31).

Biblical literature likewise distinguishes between a "singular appearance" type of ASC (e.g., to Stephen in Acts 7:55-56; to Paul in Acts 9:3-7) and a "group appearance" type (1 Cor 15:6). The singular appearance type eventually became a key element of self-understanding among the Gnostics who claimed to be receiving revelations from Jesus. The content of these revelations, however, set the Gnostics at odds with various Jesus groups. In order to preserve the value of singular appearances to Paul (which he mentioned in his letters) and to the astral prophet, John, desribed in the book of Revelation, non-Gnostic leaders set up a canon of Scripture for Jesus groups. Thereafter, no other singular visions of Jesus could have any public significance for the members of Jesus groups, particularly if the content of these visions deviated from those in the collection of normative writings, that is, the New Testament canon (Dodd 1957; Malina and Rohrbaugh 1998: 282–85).

Our knowledge of contemporary ecstatic trance experience seems to indicate that the members of a group do arrive at one and the same dimension of alternate reality. It is, however, perceived and experienced differently by each member of the group. Still, images and sometimes messages of group members overlap with those of other members of the group. It is only after each person records her or his experience and shares it with the group, that other members recognize these commonalities in the experience. The neurophysiological explanation for these commonalities makes good sense. A group that goes into trance together is experiencing the same alterations in their neurophysiological status in this shared experience. But the latent discourse, the "cultural dogma" embraced by each member differs, hence the interpretation of the experience will differ (Goodman 1973: 101).

According to the scriptural record, God raised Jesus from the dead, after which the risen Jesus appeared to his followers. The resurrection appearances reported in the Gospels can be grouped into two large categories: those that occurred at the tomb of Jesus, and those that occurred away from the tomb (Pilch 1998). In the altered states of consciousness experiences at the tomb, people—actually women—saw Jesus and other beings from the realm of God. According to anthropological and psychiatric studies, it is not uncommon for survivors to have vivid experiences of departed loved ones for up to ten years after the event and even longer. Such experiences are especially common at the burial place (Pilch 1998a).

In Acts 1:6-11, the risen Jesus appears to his disciples as he is about to depart from them. It is, therefore, a group type of appearance. Actually this is the last of many appearances to disciples during some of which the risen Jesus "ate and drank" with them (Acts 10:41). Luke has already reported one such instance in his Gospel. "While they were still incredulous for joy and were amazed, he asked them, 'Have you anything here to eat?' They gave him a piece of baked fish; he took it and ate it in front of them" (Luke 24:41-43). What are we scientifically sophisticated readers supposed to make of this? Did he really eat the fish? Some scholars have said, "Definitely not." Dead people don't need nourishment! That modern scientific Western perspective, however, misses the point of this first-century report from part of the Mediterranean world.

In his lifetime, Jesus was considered a "holy man" (Mark 1:24 "Holy One of God"). In the Israelite tradition, this is a technical term roughly equivalent to "shaman." (The Hebrew words that identify such a person are *ṣaddiq* and *ḥasid*.) In all cultures, a holy man (woman) is characterized by an ability to have ready and direct access to God and the realm of God, and to broker power and favors from that realm to human beings. This certainly describes Jesus very well. Further, the rabbinic traditions speak often about the reward for a holy man (woman) in the world to come. One tradition states that after death, the righteous enjoy in heaven meals at golden tables that have three golden legs (see *Hagig* 14b; Pilch 1998a). This explicit rabbinic tradition expecting the eating of food in the world-to-come and the implication of this imagery in Jesus' comparing the reign of God to (wedding) banquets suggests a simple answer to the question about the risen Jesus: "Did the risen Jesus [really] eat the fish?" (in Luke 24:42-43). His cultural contemporaries would have replied, "Of course he did!" Placing this discussion into the modern understanding of nutrition in human life and observing that the dead no longer have such needs ignores the latent discourse or cultural beliefs of the ancients which serve as the hermeneutical key to ASC experiences.

Anthropologists who do research on experiences in altered states of consciousness point out that reality has many dimensions beyond that of which human beings are routinely aware. Dr. Goodman distinguishes between ordinary reality and alternate reality (Gore 1995: x). Both constitute the totality of reality. Ordinary or culturally "normal" reality includes those aspects or dimensions of reality of which persons are most commonly aware most of the time. Alternate or non-ordinary reality includes those dimensions of reality in which God and the spirits are to be found. This division fits one post-Enlightenment world view, hence it forms our cultural consensus reality. Of course, some people in our culture, perhaps on the basis of "hard science" or personal experience, would even deny the existence of any alternate or non-ordinary reality.

On the other hand, for 90 percent of the population of the world, the common consensus reality embraces both ordinary and non-ordinary reality. Ordinary reality and alternate reality exist simultaneously and are part and parcel of normal experience, available to the common awareness of all members of the society. Dr. Goodman further reports that ethnography reveals that cultures believe alternate reality to be a "twin" of ordinary reality. This helps us to understand why Luke would say that the risen Jesus would request and eat baked fish. It accords perfectly with the Israelite tradition about a holy man.

Human beings live in ordinary reality and move definitively to alternate reality at death. Yet it is possible to visit alternate reality from ordinary reality in trance journeys also called "spirit or soul loss" by anthropologists. Conversely those who live in alternate reality (God, spirits, beloved departed) can and do visit ordinary reality, too. Dr. Goodman's research has discovered that cultures identify a passageway between ordinary and alternate reality (Goodman 1990: 180). It is a hole, or opening, or crack, or door between the earth and sky that the visionary must find and pass through in order to travel to alternate reality.

According to the sacred traditions of many cultures, that hole, or crack, or door, is located over the city in which the deity is said to reside, the city in which the temple is found. In the Greek tradition, the hole is over Delphi. In the Israelite tradition, the hole is over Jerusalem where the Temple was built. Before the Temple it seems God could be contacted at Babel (Gen 11:5) or at Bethel (Gen 28:17). From this perspective, Jesus could not likely have ascended to the realm of God in Galilee (Matt 28:16); the hole isn't located there. Moreover, Matthew doesn't say that Jesus ascended there, only that he met the disciples there. Luke is the only evangelist to describe the ascension of Jesus (Luke 24:50; Acts 1:6-11; the event is mentioned elsewhere though, e.g., John 20:17). He locates the event at Bethany (Luke 24:50) on the Mount of Olives (Acts 1:12). Jesus would certainly be able to find that opening between ordinary reality and alternate reality, this world and the realm of God, in the environs of Jerusalem.

But contemporary trance research and experience recognizes that the opening is not necessarily a geographical location as it is more a question of tuning the body that exists in ordinary reality to the frequency of alternate reality (Goodman 1990: 180–181). Preparation of the body for this experience involves a ritual posture, sensory (over)stimulation, heavy exertion, sleeplessness, the states of being—emotion, and the like—that accompany the loss of a loved one to death, among other strategies. Only with this special preparation of the physical self is the visionary able to properly perceive alternate reality. Research indicates that this preparation can be learned. It may be part of the general cultural expectations as in the ancient Mediterranean world, or it can be learned as in the modern Western world. As a holy man during his lifetime, Jesus obviously possessed the ability to perceive alternate reality, the realm of God. He quite likely learned how to visit it after the manner of Ezekiel (Ezek 8:3) and John the author of Revelation (Rev 1:10; 4:2; 17:3; 21:10). Plausibly, Jesus might have learned such strategies from John the Baptist, himself acknowledged as a holy man. Now after his resurrection, Jesus is ready to return to the realm of God in a way in which he has been accustomed to associating with the Father during his lifetime, namely, through ecstatic trance (e.g., Luke 3:21-22). The disciples who, as the Gospels indicate, are also capable of such experiences (e.g., Luke 9:28-36) witness the event (Acts 1:9-10).

Luke's report of Jesus' ascension includes markers of a trance experience typical in the Israelite tradition: a cloud, figures dressed in white garments, and interpretation of the experience (Acts 1:9-11). The passive voice "was lifted up" (v. 9) identifies God as the one who takes the risen Jesus to the divine realm (see also "taken up," Luke 9:51; Acts 1:2; "carried up," Luke 24:51; contrast "departure," Luke 9:31, RSV). When no human agent can be identified, the passive voice in the Bible is a way of speaking about God without using God's name. It is called a "theological passive" of a "divine passive." Visits to and residence in the realm of God require God's approval. A cloud (dark, but sometimes bright, Luke 9:34) marks God's presence (Exod 19:9; 16; 34:5; Num 11:25; Deut 4:11; Ezek 1:4, 28; 2 Sam 22:12). The two men in white robes are typical of Luke who tends to report pairs where the other evangelists list but a single person (e.g., compare Luke 24:4 with Matt 28:2). These two men in dazzling garments are angels as they are also explicitly identified in John (20:12). In other words, they are beings from alternate reality, the realm of God. They will interpret the event for the Apostles.

These same markers can also be understood with insights from cognitive neuroscience. In trance, the visionary knows from experience that he or she is in a trance state by the colors he or she sees. These colors relate directly to neurological activity. Many scientists have traced electroencephalograms (EEGs) of people who signal when they are aware of having entered a different level of consciousness. For instance, two neuroscientists have studied Franciscan religious women at prayer and Tibetan monks in meditation and analyzed the tracings carefully (Newberg and d'Aquili 2001: 7). The subjects in these studies described their experiences to the scientists who correlated their reports with the tracings on their EEG machines. Among the many things they learned about the function of the brain in these experiences is the significance of colors seen. Seeing a bright color signals a shift in consciousness or awareness. This is a sure sign of being in trance.

The anthropologist, Dr. Goodman, has developed this same insight and has taught it at The Cuyamungue Institute. The sequence of colors seen in trance reflects neurological changes. To see white is a sign of being in a trance. Orange means the trance is weakening. Naturalistic colors indicate a still weaker level of trance. To see actual distinct figures means the trance is over. What is seen in trance is hazy and indistinct. (Recall how often the risen Jesus was not recognized by those who knew him in his earthly life.) When one sees clearly, it is a sign that the visionary has returned to the level of waking (so called "normal") consciousness.

In the Israelite tradition, light is the manifestation of God's honor or glory (Isa 60:1; 62:1; Luke 2:9), that is, God's very self. The light takes the form of a cloud (Exod 24:15ff) or fire (Deut

5:24) flashing brightly (Ezek 1:4, 27-28; 10:4). The bright light from the sky (Acts 9:3; 22:6) even brighter than the sun (26:13) that Paul saw on the road to Damascus is typical of stage one of an ecstatic trance. (Anthropologists identify three stages in a typical trance experience. See Acts 9 for details.) Paul the Pharisee, familiar with the significance of light in the Israelite tradition, would be aware that he was entering a different level of awareness, a different "stage" of consciousness, or that some being from the realm of God might be initiating communication with him.

In the resurrection reports, the young man clothed in the white robe is plausibly a being from the realm of God (Mark 16:5). In Matthew, the angel of the Lord has an appearance "like lightening and his clothing was white as snow" (28:3). As indicated above, in Luke (24:4), the two men in dazzling garments are angels explicitly identified as such in John (20:12). The two men in Acts 1:9 are therefore also angels. In the resurrection reports, Jesus is never associated with the color white. (He is described in this way in the transfiguration—Matt 17:1-18 and par.) From a neurological perspective, the white color signals that the visionaries are indeed in an altered state of awareness. They are experiencing visitors from the realm of God and the spirits. In the resurrection appearances, however, he is frequently not recognized. The fact that they often don't recognize "the distinct face or figure" of Jesus further indicates this is an experience in an altered state of awareness. What is seen in trance is not a photographic image but rather a vague and indistinct figure.

Every vision, every trance experience needs an interpretation. This is quite evident in reports of prophetic visions (e.g., Jer 1:11-19). At the ascension of Jesus, the angels interpret for the Apostles what they have seen in trance. "This Jesus who has been taken up from you into heaven will return in the same way as you have seen him going into heaven" (Acts 1:11). So this departure of Jesus for the realm of God will be followed at some time in the future by his return in like manner.

Between those two events, however, the apostles and their followers are to be *witnesses* "in Jerusalem, throughout Judea and Samaria, and to the ends of the earth" (Acts 1:8). The witness they are to bear is much more than a simple testimony to events. Luke has delineated the purpose of witnessing at the end of his Gospel. The risen Jesus reminds his disciples of all that was written about him in the Torah, the Prophets, and the Psalms that must be fulfilled. "Repentance, for the forgiveness of sins, [should] be preached in [Jesus'] name to all the nations, beginning from Jerusalem" (Luke 24:44-49). The Apostles are therefore to communicate the fuller understanding of what the Scriptures say about Jesus Messiah. Scholars agree that these verses of interpretation are probably not verbatim reports from the visionaries but more likely Lucan creations. That makes no difference to our interpretation.

The Apostles experienced Jesus' return to the realm of God in an altered state of consciousness experience. Either in that very experience, or some time later in the community that grew around them, the Apostles became emboldened to preach their fuller understanding of Jesus, an understanding gained in their altered states of consciousness experiences.

For reflection:

1. From their study of the human brain and nervous system, cognitive neuro-scientists have concluded that God has incredibly "hard-wired" the human body for ASC experiences. How can one learn more about the function of the brain and nervous system in religious experience? What might one do to develop these abilities rather than short circuit them?

2. The disciples as a group experienced the risen Jesus on more than one occasion after the resurrection. This is a group-type vision. Can you imagine or do you know a group of believers with whom you would be able to experience the risen Jesus? What might be the occasion? How might the group prepare itself for such an experience?

3. Have you ever experienced something in prayerful meditation that didn't make sense at the time of prayer but later when you gained understanding it did make sense? How might this type of experience help to understand ecstatic trance?

Acts 1:12-26 Replacing Judas

No altered states of consciousness event is reported in this section, but a related concept is, namely, basing a decision on lots. "Then they gave lots to them [Joseph and Matthias], and the lot fell upon Matthias, and he was counted with the eleven apostles" (Act 1:26). God must choose which of these two candidates (Matthias or Joseph) should succeed Judas. But how does one learn God's will? One way is when God reveals it in an altered state of consciousness experience, a trance. One night Paul had a vision (perhaps a dream) of a man inviting him to come to Macedonia. Paul interpreted this as God's call to proclaim the good news there (Acts 16:9-10). Joseph betrothed to Mary learned God's will in a dream (Matt 1:20-23). Other mediums through which people learn God's will include "the angel of the Lord" (one of the four: Gabriel, Raphael, Michael, and Uriel; Matt 1:20), the stars in the sky (Ezekiel; Revelation), and Scripture (Matt 2:4-6). The instructions come at God's initiative.

Sometimes humans could take the initiative to invite God to communicate the divine intention. People known to have access to God like prophets or holy men or holy women could be requested to seek God's will for another person. King Saul visited the medium at Endor for this purpose (see 1 Sam 28:7-8) but only after seeking God's advice personally, directly, yet unsuccessfully in dreams and in lots (1 Sam 28:6).

Lots in the ancient world were one strategy for divination, for discerning God's will. This practice was rooted in the belief that God (or the gods) was in control of life and responsible for everything. One should not act unless one is as certain as can be that one is acting according to God's will. One form of lots is ridiculed by the prophet Hosea (4:12). People would appeal to Allat, the "lady of the rod," using short pieces of stick with bark on one side and bare wood on the other. They were thrown like dice and turning up the bare side was a good omen. Some contemporary Middle Easterners write upon sticks "God bids" and "God forbids," and then draw from them to determine God's will.

What were these lots that the Apostles used? Scholars know next to nothing about the origin or the method of this process. Some suggest it was using two pebbles or other materials that could be identified as a positive or negative response, "yes" or "no." If so, this strategy was similar to that behind the Urim and Thummim strategy, which was used by the priests (Num 27:21). While to the Western mind, this sounds like "chance," to the Middle Eastern mind the outcome was indeed God's will (Josh 18:8; 21:8). Peter's comments suggest that this was indeed this community's belief about the lot. First, God is definitely in control. Judas met his fate in fulfillment of Scripture (God's will; Acts 1:16). He was "allotted a share" (v. 17) but forfeited it. Now the Apostles, or more precisely God, will have to select a successor to Judas. This successor should have been "with us the whole time the Lord Jesus came and went among us" from the baptism until the day he was "taken up from us" (Acts 1:21-22). With this passing comment, Peter indicates that the group at the ascension of Jesus was larger than the Eleven. In fact, since these two candidates are proposed as being at the ascension, it was at least thirteen! With only two candidates from which to choose, the lot system ("yes" and "no") worked effectively. But the choice would not be simple "fate." The prayer of Peter (Acts 1:24-25) makes it clear that God will make the choice. God acts by means of the lot, and it is God's will that Matthias should replace Judas.

For reflection:

1. How do modern believers discern the will of God? Is there a method or a process? Is there more than one method or process? Can there be a faulty discernment process that only serves to reinforce the believer's will rather than God's? What certainty can modern believers attribute to having truly discerned God's will?

2. Selection of a successor to Judas highlights a certain degree of cooperation between human beings and God. In other words, as the rabbinic tradition teaches, God's will entails 100% of human effort and 100% of divine implementation. The Apostles established criteria for a successor to Judas and offered God alternatives. Does this sound like a reliable process of discerning God's will in the modern world? How might it work?

ACTS 2:1-47 PENTECOST

Acts 2 is a literary unit focused on Pentecost. It is also bounded by an *inclusio,* or literary bookends, in v. 2 (RSV): "the day" and in v. 41: "that day."

Acts 2:1-13 Outpouring of the Spirit

Acts 2:1-4 Group ASC experience of the descent of the Spirit

While the group was gathered, it experienced a "noise like a strong driving wind" (v. 2) and "tongues as of fire" (v. 3). Luke explains that they were all filled with the "holy Spirit" (v. 4). It is important to remember that the Hebrew and Greek words translated "spirit" *(ruah; pneuma)* can also be translated as "wind" or "breath." Luke uses a different Greek word for "driving wind" *(pnoe),* which is quite likely what the actual experience might have been. Luke, however, interprets this as a "holy wind," that is, a "holy Spirit." Our ancestors in faith did not distinguish between natural and supernatural. That distinction first emerged with Origen in the third century A.D. Prior to Origen, the realm of God and God's angels, spirits, demons, genies, stars, and planets were all part of the total environment in which human beings lived. This was the totality of reality. Spirits could and did regularly interfere in human life. People were always on the lookout for that. Since the ancients had no notion of impersonal causality (e.g., there is no phrase in Hebrew for "it rained"; rather, God sends the rain, God withholds the rain, etc.) every event had to have a personal cause. Therefore, every significant effect, every effect that is significant in human life is caused by a person. So if something significant happens, one asks "who did it?" rather than "what did it?" If no human person could be identified, then the cause was likely another than human person. Hence this driving wind sent by God could be interpreted as a holy Spirit.

The Israelites wore talismans (usually blue in color, but also purple and scarlet among other colors) to keep the spirits at bay (see Exod 35:35). The reason for the range of colors is that purple comes from the sea anemone. This dye runs the range from crimson through red to purple. It was not a fast color, so anything dyed from this dye was considered purple (Pilch 1999: 19). The concern was whether a spirit was good, bad, or just capricious. The Gospels report people possessed and tormented by varieties of bad, impure, or evil spirits (e.g., Luke 8:27). Whatever the nature of a spirit, it was powerful. The spirit or wind of God hovered over the primordial waters and put order into the chaos (Gen 1). The spirit of the LORD came upon Samson and he killed a lion bare-handed (Judg 14:6) and thirty able-bodied men singlehandedly (Judg 14:19). The spirit of the LORD came upon Mary and she became pregnant (Matt 1:18). The last instance is explicitly explained as the activity of a good spirit. This background helps understand why Luke could interpret a "strong driving wind" as a "holy Spirit."

The quest for the "factual event" behind this report can be assisted by viewing it as another group type experience of ecstatic trance. Whether Luke has created the story, or embellished a tradition, it is best understood and interpreted as an altered states of consciousness experience shared by a group. Luke mentions two elements in this group type trance: auditory and visual, or sound and vision. The sound comes from the sky, hence it presumably has an other than human source. The Israelite tradition considered thunder to be the voice of God (Ps 29; Mark 1:11), though people could differ in their interpretation of the sounds they heard. When Jesus prayed to his Father, a voice responded from the sky. Some of the bystanders said it had thundered, others said an angel spoke to him. Jesus heard intelligible words from God (John 12:29). Here in Acts, Luke supplies the interpretation: it is the sound of a strong, driving wind descending from the sky and filling the entire house where the people were sitting. The wind originates in the sky, the realm of God. God is the agent in this event.

The visual element in this group trance is "tongues as of fire." These objects would probably be of red color, perhaps tinged with yellow. As already noted above, colors perceived in altered states of consciousness help identify different levels of the neurophysiological events. These colors indicate that the group definitely is in trance. It may be a weak one, but it is trance nonetheless. The shape of the fire (tongues) can indicate two things. The tongues resemble a geometric pattern that characterizes the first stage of trance. In the second stage, the visionary attempts to make sense of the patterns by imposing shape upon them. Considering the glossolalia that this experience produces, it is possible that the tongue shape (interpretation) was imposed on the geometric patterns after the fact, that is, after the experience of speaking in tongues (glossolalia). It is also possible that the geometric patterns suggested images of tongues that then contributed to or prompted the glossolalia.

Luke reports that the Spirit enabled the gathered people to speak "in different tongues" (glossalalia; Acts 2:4). Peter's speech interprets the phenomenon as speaking "other languages" (xenoglossy; Acts 2:6, 8). Dr. Goodman's published research into the contemporary experience of glossolalia is very instructive here (Goodman 1972). She studied the phenomenon as tape recorded by other researchers among diverse groups including the Umbanda Spiritualist Cult in Brazil, elements of which Brazilian Catholics have syncretistically incorporated into their own prayer rituals. Goodman conducted her personal research in a Spanish speaking Pentecostal congregation in Mexico City and a Mayan speaking branch of the same church in Yucatan (Goodman 2001: 8, 125, 187 on xenoglossy). In glossolalia, speech becomes musical sound. Glossolalia, she observed, is lexically non-communicative. This is not the informative or communicative side of discourse.

Though some, as in Luke's report here, think they are hearing a foreign language (technically called xenoglossy), it is highly unlikely that this ever occurs. In Yucatan, Goodman noticed that the congregation began to develop its own glossolalia dialect, different from that of its leader and his assistant. Listening to the tape later, the congregation did not recognize its own glossolalia. Thus, perception in the altered states of consciousness apparently did not carry over into ordinary waking consciousness. What remained constant, however, was the rhythmic pattern of speech and the identical intonation curve that can be heard on all tape recordings, no matter where they are made (Goodman 2001: 137).

Other important insights from Goodman's research are that those she studied broke into glossolalia only while in an altered states of consciousness (Goodman 2001: 136). Those who received glossolalia customarily considered it proof of a factual presence of the Holy Spirit. Of course, this impresses those who are observers and embarrasses group members who fail to produce glossolalia under the appropriate circumstances. Most of the time, glossolalia is learned. The leader of the group offers a pattern for others to imitate and they do (see 1 Sam 5:1-10). Even so, Goodman observed an instance where a complete stranger wandered into a community in trance, heard the glossolalia, dissociated and produced a vocalisation, and then disappeared. The group concluded that it was indeed the work of the Spirit. However, the result is a concern about this person who has come too close to the mystery of God without proper "protection" or "immunity" from possible divine displeasure. Israelite members of Jesus groups who witnessed non-Israelites experiencing ecstatic utterance within their midst may well have considered this a gift of God that put the unbaptized recipient at grave risk without baptism; hence, they were quickly baptized (Acts 10:44-48). Dr. Goodman has noted that many cultures consider contact with the realm of the deity to be a blessing but also one filled with great risk. (The custom of "churching" women after the birth of a child in pre-Second Vatican Council Catholicism has its roots in this belief: the mother has come perilously close to the mystery of life and must be "regularized" again through a suitable rite.)

Luke's description of these gathered people as speaking in "different tongues" (Acts 2:4) and later different languages (Acts 2:6, 8) can be explained in a number of ways. One explanation is that Luke has misunderstood the event (Esler 1992: 141). Perhaps he was insufficiently familiar with glossolalia as patterned speech and accepted the tradition behind this event as it was given. Some of the groups Goodman studied did believe that they were speaking true languages in trance that a native might understand if present. She concluded that that was highly unlikely (Goodman 2001: 187).

Notice that in his list of gifts bestowed by God upon the community in Corinth around A.D. 54, Paul put speaking in and interpreting tongues last. It would seem that the Corinthian community may have been making too much of this gift. Paul reacted in the same way that later church leaders reacted to Gnostic claims based on trance experiences that were at odds with the basic tradition. At the time when Luke wrote Acts (around A.D. 80-85), ecstatic utterance may well have been completely checked by the community and occurred but rarely if at all. This would account for Luke's or the tradition's misinterpretation of speaking in tongues as speaking in foreign languages. Other scholars think Luke may have made reference to "different languages" deliberately to demonstrate the reversal of the confusion of languages at Babel (Gen 11:1-9). The main point, however, remains unchanged: this group of people is experiencing the Spirit in an altered state of consciousness. Everything described (except for the misinterpretation of the nature of what is being said) is consonant with trance experiences.

This Jerusalem group broke into ecstatic utterance when they became aware of being empowered by a mighty Spirit. The limited visual element reported by the community (tongues as of fire is all they saw) is also consonant with a trance in which ecstatic utterance occurs. The primary experience in a trance involving singing, chanting, or other sound is euphoria and peace. The visuals are not as rich and plentiful as in other kinds of trance. Ecstatic utterance trance is a very somatic rather than cerebral experience. There rarely are messages or insights. One is happy just to be in this state and is reluctant to leave it.

For reflection:

1. Read John 12:27-30. How did the different people interpret the sound that was heard? If you had been present, what do you think you would have heard and interpreted?

2. In Acts 2:1-4, Luke intentionally notes that the group experiences the Spirit now in a domestic dwelling rather than in the Jerusalem Temple. The locale for experiencing God is shifting from Temple (political religion) to home (domestic religion). Where do contemporary believers experience the Spirit?

3. How do modern believers report experiences of "speaking in tongues"? How does the experienced named "being slain in the Spirit" compare?

Acts 2:5-13 Group trance experience of glossolalia

The group in trance are Galileans who could be distinguished from Judeans by the regional peculiarities of their pronunciation of Aramaic. They must have gone out of the house in which they were located. Luke imagines that their ecstatic behavior and utterances could not help but attract the attention of the Judean locals and Israelite visitors to Jerusalem. Sophisticated Jerusalemites no doubt held the popular stereotype of Galileans, their Northern neighbors, as backwater "boorish dolts." This culture of collectivistic personalities routinely stereotypes all people. (Eighty percent of the contemporary world population are collectivistic personalities.) This tendency would explain their skepticism, not about the event but about how it was induced: "They have had too much new wine" (Acts 2:13). In contrast, devout members of the house of Israel from every nation under heaven were amazed to hear these Galileans telling "the mighty acts of God" (v. 11).

The conflicting judgments of these devout believers reflects what contemporary research shows, namely, that trance is actually part of a wide spectrum of human experience that includes the alteration of consciousness caused by consumption of alcohol. The ancients knew this as well. "Those who linger long over wine. / . . . / Your eyes behold strange sights, / and your heart utters disordered thoughts" (Prov 23:30, 33). The skeptics heard the glossolalia but interpreted it as "disordered thoughts" produced by drunkenness. They did not deny the altered state of consciousness. They concluded that it was induced by wine and produced gibberish. The devout members of the House of Israel heard the visionaries reporting "the mighty acts of God" (Acts 1:11) and concluded that the trance and ecstatic utterances were God-induced and God-inspired.

Paul indicates that ecstatic utterance is unintelligible to those producing it (1 Cor 12–14). It requires interpretation (1 Cor 12:10), a gift from God for which a believer can pray (1 Cor 14:3). Contemporary trance experience is very similar. The ideal facilitator(s) of groups who practice trance or the visionaries themselves are those who have a grasp of the latent discourse of the culture and/or of their respective religious tradition. In the following verses, Luke crafts a speech for

Peter that will interpret the group trance experience for the listeners, which includes the visionaries.

Geographically, the specific regions mentioned in vv. 9-11 form something like a box around Judea-Jerusalem signaling the beginnings of the fulfillment of the expanding mission announced in Acts 1:8. Yet the people involved are all of the house of Israel: pilgrims, immigrants, and proselytes. We must move further into Acts to witness movement toward the Samaritans and the non-Israelites.

For reflection:

1. About 80% of the world's cultures are collectivistic while 20% are individualistic. Collectivistic cultures hold congregating values; individualistic cultures hold isolating values. Collectivistic personalities are closely attached to their groups; individualistic personalities strive to stand apart from their groups. These two different personality types have two different types of trance experiences: "group types," that is, a group shares a trance experience (e.g., Acts 1:6-11) and "singular types," that is, an individual has a personal trance experience (e.g., Acts 9:3-6). Of course, both types of experience are available in both cultures. Which type would you prefer? Why?

2. The contrasting responses to the group type experience reported in this segment raise a good question. How would members of a group determine whether the groups' experience is "wine induced" or "God induced"? Would an authoritative word from someone who was not present at the experience help? What qualifications ought those officials who investigate such experiences possess?

Acts 2:14-36 Interpreting the group trance experience

"What does this mean?" (Acts 2:12). Human beings are meaning-seeking creatures. They cannot live without meaning, without understanding. Altered states of consciousness experiences are non-linear. They need to be sorted out and interpreted. In this event, Peter, who is one of the visionaries and glossolalists, sets forth an explanation. Specialists in Acts of the Apostles point out that Luke has created these speeches for various characters in Acts. This is the first of six. Five are spoken by Peter (Acts 3:12-26; 4:8-12; 5:29-32; 10:34-43), and one by Paul (13:16-41). All center on the meaning of the resurrection of Jesus. Even if this speech is a Lucan creation, in the storyline it presents an interpretation of the altered states of consciousness experience just witnessed by many in Jerusalem. Typical of such explanations, this one, too, is rooted in the latent discourse of the culture, the Israelite tradition that was familiar to Luke and certainly fit quite appropriately on the lips of Peter.

First, Peter denies that the visionaries are drunk. He insists that what has occurred has been the work of God foretold by the prophet Joel (Acts 2:14-16). Placed as it is in the very first speech in Acts (2:17-21), the citation from Joel (3:1-5) indicates at the very least that altered states of consciousness experiences such as the one just witnessed will be repeated as the life and story of the community continues. Luke has creatively rearranged and reinterpreted the citation.

> It will come to pass in the last days
> A that I will pour out . . . my spirit
> B sons and daughters will prophesy
>   C young men will see visions
>   Old men shall dream dreams
> B' upon my servants and handmaids
> A' I will pour out . . . my spirit.
>
> (Acts 2:17-18, authors's translation)

The promise of the fifth century B.C.E. prophet ("in those [forthcoming] days") is actualized by Peter: "in the last days." The central section, C, of these concentrically arranged verses are Peter's main point: visions and dreams, that is, ecstatic trance experiences will continue. It is noteworthy that these

there a leader or facilitator in the group? What role does he or she play? (Viewing the video "Macumba" can substitute for a visit to such a religious community.)

2. In the Greek Old Testament, God's two great, mighty deeds are creation (giving life) and salvation or redemption (restoring meaning to life). John's Gospel uses the same Greek word *(erga)* for Jesus' mighty deeds which he calls "signs." Jesus' seven mighty deeds or "signs" (the same word *semeion*, "sign," is added to the Joel text noted above) can be clustered into two groups: deeds that give life (John 4:46-54; 6:1-15; 11:38-44) and deeds that restore meaning to life (John 2:1-1; 5:1-9; 6:16-21; 9:1-8). How can modern believers contribute to giving life and enriching the meaning of life—to themselves and to others? What is the role of the Spirit in such activity?

Acts 2:37-47 Regrouping

The response to Peter's speech is incredible. His promise is certainly tempting. If they repent and are baptized, they will obtain forgiveness for the great crime they have committed against God and God's Messiah, but they will also receive the gift of the holy Spirit. This is the same Spirit who is responsible for the marvelous experience of glossolalia that they had witnessed. Moreover, the promise of the Spirit is to those present ("you") and their children, and to "whomever the Lord our God will call." Again, says Luke, Peter reminds us that God is in charge and in control. God determines to whom and when to give the Spirit. God is in charge of the community's growth (vv. 41, 47). Even if the number is inflated (three thousand), a sizable group of persons who witnessed the event and heard the speech repented, submitted to baptism, and joined the fledgling group that very day.

Verses 42-47 are the first of three major generalizing summaries in Acts (4:32-35 and 5:11-16; short summaries are 5:42; 9:31; 12:24; 15:35; 19:20). Stylistically these were useful to Luke because of the fragmentary nature of his information. The summary tends to highlight the usual and typical traits of the period just described. This summary describes the rules of community that new members were expected to observe. They probably describe community life at Luke's time. It speaks of impressive unity in the community that all scholars recognize as an idealization. Anyone remotely familiar with life in Mediterranean culture knows it is agonistic, that is, argumentative and combative, even within families and certainly within fictive kinship groups such as this community as well. Perhaps the idealization also reflects the author's distance from the events he is describing.

Fidelity to the Apostles' teaching guarantees the continuity between Jesus and his Apostles and those who follow. Breaking of bread is likely a technical term in Acts for Eucharist (v. 64; 20:7, 11; 27:35). Wonders and signs point ahead to the next section (Acts 3:1-11) where the work of the Spirit continues. Reference to meeting in the Temple and in private homes also points ahead where eventually this union will be broken. While the house of Israel to this point has been open to the message about Jesus, the Messiah, it will soon turn hostile. The important point is the very last statement. God is in control of the life and growth of this community.

For reflection:

1. As good as it may be in some cultures and in some individuals, human memory in general tends to reinterpret and often idealize events that had very different origins. Luke is reporting events he did not witness and experiences of people he quite likely never met, hence never interviewed. How ought a reader receive and interpret this idealizing summary?

2. Our ancestors in faith were convinced God was in control of everything that happened. How do modern believers understand or interpret the role of God in control of the community's life?

Chapter 2

Acts 3–5
Temple Tours

God Acts in the Temple and a Private Home

We noted that chapter 1 was framed by bookends, or an inclusion. These chapters are also framed by two references to temple and house settings. "Every day they devoted themselves to meeting together in the temple area and to breaking bread in their homes" (Acts 2:46). "And all day long, both at the temple and in their homes, they did not stop teaching and proclaiming the Messiah, Jesus" (Acts 5:42). Most of the activity takes place in the Temple area (3:1–4:22 and 5:12-41). In between these frames is a brief description of activities peculiar to the internal life of the community away from the Temple, especially in a home setting (4:23–5:11). In other words, while the young community continues to pray in the Temple (Acts 3:1), the true "place" of prayer is the "place in which they were gathered," a home (Acts 4:31). Luke is apparently beginning to point to the shift away from the Temple, which is criticized by Stephen in Acts 7, to the home, the new center of religious community (Elliott 1991: 211–40).

ACTS 3:1–4:22 PUBLIC TEMPLE TOUR: GOD ACTS IN THE TEMPLE

Acts 3:1-10 Healing in ecstatic trance

The setting of this scene is "the Beautiful Gate" (vv. 2, 10), which is likely the gate of Nicanor that leads from the Court of the non-Israelites into the Court of the women. In other words, the healing takes place within the Temple precincts just outside the Temple building proper. Readers who have seen photographs of the Temple mount must remember that only the small (in size) but tall building (relative to all other structures on the site) is the actual Temple. Access to it was quite restricted and non-Israelites were warned not to approach the Temple building. To be this close indicates that the man must have been an Israelite.

If the Beautiful Gate is indeed the gate of Nicanor as archaeologists suggest, it was made of Corinthian bronze. The lame man begging by the Beautiful Gate illustrates what Luke's Jesus said about the Temple and its personnel during his lifetime. Observing a poor widow drop her two small coins into the Temple treasury, Jesus noted how she "from her poverty, has offered her whole livelihood" (Luke 21:4). Why did she do such a foolish thing? Because she was so instructed by religious leaders (scribes) who "devour the houses of widows and, as a pretext, recite lengthy prayers" (Luke 20:47). The Temple and its personnel were to collect offerings and redistribute them to the needy. Instead, they spent them on conspicuous consumption ("long robes . . . seats of honor in synagogues, and places of honor at banquets" Luke 20:46). The lame man was ignored by individuals passing by who had surplus and scorned by political religious authorities who definitely had such surplus. Recall the Pharisee who boasted of his tithes but distanced himself from needy people (Luke 18:9-14).

It is almost impossible to identify the exact maladies of sick people in the Bible, but descriptions make it clear that lameness is a compromised ability to walk or otherwise use one's limbs. That is clearly the case here. Quite likely the family of the man who was lame from birth brought him daily to this advantageous entry point to the Temple where he begged alms (v. 2). Spotting Peter and John as they entered the Temple, the man asked for alms. What follows next is very significant. Peter "looked intently" at him (v. 4). The Greek verb *atenizo* can also be translated "gaze" or "stare." This word appears just fourteen times in the New Testament. Luke uses it twelve times and of these, ten occur in Acts. Paul uses it twice (2 Cor 3:7, 13).

Australian biblical scholar Rick Strelan (2000: 492) observes some significance to the usage of this verb. In most of the instances in which the verb occurs, it signals an altered state of consciousness experience. What are the indications of this? First, the subject is a holy person, that is a *ṣaddiq* or *ḥasid* (see above p. 4; and Pilch 1998). God customarily communicates with holy persons in an altered state or consciousness (1 Sam 3:1). This passage would appear to be the first indication that Peter and John were recognized as holy men. As such, they would have direct access to God and the ability to broker favors from God to other human beings. This may well be the immediate result of receiving the Spirit just shortly before this at the Pentecost event. Surely Jesus, whom each knew intimately and with whom they associated in his life on earth, would seek this gift for them from the Father. Recall the Mediterranean cultural trait of favoritism toward family and friends.

Second, the subject of this verb is at prayer or in trance. Since Peter and John were going specifically to the Temple for the "three o'clock hour of prayer" (v. 1), they could already have been praying as they walked. It is not unusual among modern Jews, especially in the Conservative and Orthodox traditions, to pray in synagogue, turn to greet or converse with others, and return to prayer. The activity is seamless. It is also the case in Catholic congregations after the consecration at the Liturgy during which time their attention is most intensely focused on the mysteries to turn shortly afterwards to other worshipers and share a greeting of peace.

But perhaps the more plausible explanation is that Peter and John induced the trance when they heard the lame man's request for alms. This is easily done especially in a culture where altering states of consciousness intentionally or unintentionally is second nature. One is enculturated in the technique and appropriate rite. Indeed, gazing or staring or looking intently (as we shall see in other instances in Acts) might not only be the sign of being in trance but also a technique for inducing trance, a part of the requisite rite. From the perspective of cognitive neuroscience, such intense concentration can induce a trance "from the top down." This level of consciousness originates primarily in the brain either by clearing the mind of all thoughts or focusing intensely on a thought (d'Aquili and Newberg 1999: 114–18). Peter and John are intently focused on the lame man, and this level of concentration very plausibly put them into an altered state of consciousness.

Luke uses a different Greek word to describe the lame man's response. "He paid attention to them, expecting to receive something from them" (v. 5). Likely the man is not initially in trance. He is looking to see what they will give him. But since the word can be translated as "gaze," it is possible that when he perceived Peter and John in trance ("looking at him intently") he might also have been drawn into the trance. This does happen in cultures where trance is a recognized medium for healing. Judging by the external appearances of trance, the petitioner realizes the holy man is indeed in communion with the realm of God and is drawn into it him or herself.

Third, the person "gazing" or "staring" has an intuition that he realizes could not and does not come from the evidence at hand, from "ordinary" reality. What is the intuition? It is the insight given by the Spirit in trance, that while Peter and John have no alms to give the petitioner, they can gift him with something better since they are aware of being for the moment in alternate reality, in the realm of God, where the risen Jesus at God's right hand is able to broker God's healing to petitioners. "I, the LORD, am your healer" (Exod 15:26). Jesus can broker God's healing power to Peter and John for the benefit of this lame man. Ultimately, Peter is the one who does it. He raises the man up, and the man enters the Temple with them "walking and jumping and praising God" (v. 8).

How did Luke imagine what exactly happened to this man? Obviously the lame man regained mobility. Whereas previously he had to be carried and placed here, he can now walk and jump. Contemporary medical specialists admit that in this case and in many other reports the evidence is too meager to make a definitive judgment about the nature of the disability, hence also about the nature of the improvement. The question is whether the man was really lame from birth or whether Luke or the previous tradition enhanced the severity of the man's condition. If he was factually congenitally lame, club foot (talipes) is a plausible interpretation of the condition. If he became lame later in life, then perhaps the man was suffering from a psychological conversion type disorder, a "hysterical paralysis" similar to conditions Jesus had healed in his lifetime (Howard 2001: 201–5).

Peter's action in this story is identified by modern medicine as an abreactive technique, a strategy for helping such people overcome their disorder. Even if that is the case, the report of Peter's healing of a lame man for Luke shows that Peter continues the healing activity of Jesus who aided the lame (see Luke 5:17-28). Luke regularly reports health problems of exceptionally long standing in order to highlight the power of God in impossible cases. The man's entering and "jumping" in the Temple with Peter (Act 3:8) confirms the prophecy of Isaiah: "Then will the lame leap like a stag. . . ." (35:6). The people are duly impressed.

For reflection:

1. Medical anthropology distinguishes between curing a disease (remedying a pathological condition) and healing an ill-

ness (restoring meaning to life). The lame man who was barred from the Temple by his disability (Lev 21:16-24) can now enter and join the community. What aspect of his life was cured? How do you know? What aspect was healed? How do you know?

Acts 3:11-26 Preaching:
Interpreting the healing event

All altered states of consciousness experience require interpretation. The best interpreter is the visionary. Peter's interpretation of the healing that took place in trance, says Luke, is addressed to those who had witnessed the event. Peter asks: "why do you look so intently at us . . ." (v. 12). Luke uses the same Greek word to describe the gaze or stare he directed to the lame man. Did he imagine the crowd to be in trance? Did he think that it is possible that some may have been drawn into the altered state of consciousness experience depending on how close they were standing, what they saw or heard of the process, etc.? It is more likely that Luke thinks of the crowd as simply staring at Peter in amazement over what they just saw. A familiar lame man is now walking.

Just as at the Pentecost event, so, too, here according to Luke Peter offers the interpretation of what happened and directs judgment and exhortation at the witnesses. The interpretation is that God is ultimately the agent of the healing that was effected by Peter through faith in Jesus' name. Name, of course, stands for person. In the present context, name and power are related (Acts 4:7). The healing power is that with which God invested the risen Jesus who brokers this gift to those who need it through the instrumentality of his Apostles. Thus does Jesus continue to be present and helpful on earth among those who believe in him. According to Luke this is what Peter learned in his earlier trance experience at Pentecost, and the healing is what he was chosen to effect in this experience.

Peter is said to draw further conclusions. This risen Jesus, of course, is a living confrontation of the witnesses, Israelites

(Acts 3:12), with their guilt. "YOU denied the Holy and Righteous One . . . the Author of life YOU put to death" (Acts 3:14-
15, author's translation). They did this even in the face of
Pilate's offer to release Jesus. But there is hope because they
and their leaders acted in ignorance. If they repent and convert
now, their sins will be taken away. Moreover, God will send the
appointed Messiah (a reference to the expected imminent Second Coming) to them.

Drawing on tradition, the cultural latent discourse in which
visionaries find insight for interpreting their trance experiences, Luke's Peter looks to Isaiah, Moses, and Abraham. With
an allusion to one of the Servant songs, Peter points out that
the God of our ancestors "has glorified his servant Jesus" (Acts
3:13; compare Isa 52:13–53:12; see also Acts 2:26). Jesus also fits
the portrait of the long awaited Moses-like prophet (Acts 3:22-
23; Deut 18:15-20). Finally Jesus is the true descendent of Abraham (Acts 3:25) who obediently fulfills the covenant on which
previous descendants of Abraham defaulted. Jesus can "bless
you by turning each of you from your evil ways" (Acts 3:26).

For reflection:

1. Where would one go to learn more about the tradition so
that one might be in a better position to interpret experiences
in altered states of consciousness? What sources might one
consult? Would reading the Bible be a good place to begin?

2. Do you see any connection between some of the crowd
being drawn into religious trance to what happens to a crowd at
rock concerts? What might be similar? What might be different?

Acts 4:1-22 Defending the healing

True to the pattern of response to mighty deeds in the
Gospels, opinion in Acts is divided. Some are impressed and
convinced. "Many of those who heard the word came to believe and [the] number of men grew to [about] five thousand"
(Acts 4:4). Others are unmoved, skeptical, or even hostile. The

high priestly class, leaders, scribes, captain of the Temple guard, and Sadducees confronted Peter and John and detained them overnight. All of these leaders are associated with the Temple and understandably concerned about power. They wield it, and they alone delegate it. Their question "by what power or by what name have you done this?" (Acts 4:7) is serious. Power is central to politics, and unlawful use of power is treasonous, a threat to existing authority. The Temple is above all a political institution. Moreover, the Sadducees who denied the resurrection are obviously threatened by claims that God raised Jesus from the dead and "in his name this man stands before you healed" (Acts 4:10). How can they deny the resurrection of Jesus when they cannot deny the healing?

Peter repeats what he has already said (Acts 3:12-16). It was by the power and in the name of Jesus, Messiah of Nazareth, whom THEY crucified but God raised from the dead that the lame man was healed (Acts 4:10). Further, this Jesus is the stone these Temple builders rejected. If they reject Jesus, they risk toppling the massive stone Temple structure (Acts 4:11; see Psalm 118:22; compare Luke 20:17-19).

These authorities are not persuaded but are forced to release Peter and John for a few reasons. First, they are impressed that these "uneducated, ordinary" companions of Jesus spoke so boldly. Second, the people sided with Peter and John, and that was something to reckon with. The people gave praise to God for acting through Peter and John, thus confirming their claim to be messengers of God (Acts 4:19-21). Moreover, in a culture that believed all goods are limited, increase in membership of the Jesus group meant a decrease among the followers of these "leaders" of the people. It would be suicidal to aggravate this loss even further. Finally, the presence of the healed man silenced them (Acts 4:14). Mention that the man had been lame for forty years (Acts 4:27) serves two purposes. One is, as already noted, Luke's penchant for making health conditions of longer duration. Another purpose is an allusion to the Exodus and a national tradition. Israel stumbled through the desert for forty years before reaching the Promised land under the leadership of Moses. For Luke, the Israel of Peter's time faces the same possibility of redemption if and only if it follows the lead of Jesus, the prophet like Moses who brings salvation not only to this lame man but to all who call upon his name.

For reflection:

1. Though they denied the resurrection (in general), the Sadducees were an authoritative group in Judaism at that time, very powerful in relationship to the Temple. How can leaders who are so mistaken remain in such powerful control?

2. How can leadership be encouraged to maintain credibility and authority be being faithful to the "truth"? How do you discern "truth"?

ACTS 4:23–5:11 AWAY FROM THE TEMPLE:
PRIVATE HOUSE INTERLUDE

The Apostles returned to their own fictive kinship network to report their experience. This notice may be Luke's strategy for moving the story forward. Since the Apostles' experience was quite public, news of it surely reached this group by means of the gossip network (Rohrbaugh 2001; Duling 2002). The two scenes that comprise this section reveal both the unity ("with one accord" Acts 4:24) and disunity (Acts 5:1-11) in the community.

Acts 4:23-31 Response in prayer

Clearly a Lucan composition, this prayer flowing from a reflection on Psalm 2:1-2 includes a negative assessment of Herod and Pilate that differs from the report in the Gospel. Here they are lumped with the non-Israelites and Israelites as gathered against the Messiah, Jesus. In the Gospel, both are acknowledged as attempting to set Jesus free (Luke 23:15-16).

The point, however, is simply that the community prays to God, recognizing that God the "Sovereign Lord" is truly in control of the entire cosmos, not just human events. Everything happens according to God's will. The community asks for divine empowerment to continue to speak "with [all] boldness" and to continue healing and performing signs and wonders through the name of Jesus. God's response to the prayer is immediate: the house shakes and all are filled with the empowering holy Spirit (v. 31). It is reasonable to conclude that the community slipped into an altered state of consciousness during their prayer. Some trance experiences produce kinesthetic results more so than visual experiences (Gore 1995: 37; 136), and that seems to be the case here. They could feel the place shake and continued to speak the word of God with boldness (not necessarily glossolalia).

Acts 4:32–5:11 Disciplining

On the one hand, the community continues the harmonious and solicitous life earlier described (Acts 2:44-45). From one perspective, this is not extraordinary. The community reflects the ideals of friendship in the Greek world. "Friends' goods are common property" (Aristotle, *Nichomachean Ethics* 8.9.1-2). The Israelite community was to behave in similar fashion. "Open your hand to your poor and needy kinsman in your country" (Deut 15:11). In the community that lived at Qumran, once the novice had undergone a year's probation and been accepted into the community, "his property and earnings shall be handed over to the Bursar of the Congregation who shall register it to his account and shall not spend it for the Congregation" (1Q VI:19-20). Then, after another year, his property became part of the community's possessions (1Q VI:22). Here in Acts 4:36, a certain Joseph is put forth as illustrative. He is a Levite who contrasts with an uncaring counterpart in a parable (Luke 10:32). He is also one of the diaspora members of the House of Israel who came to Jerusalem for this feast.

Voluntarily he disposed of property and gave it to the Apostles to distribute as necessary.

On the other hand, not all community members practiced this ideal. Two, Ananias and Sapphira, a husband and wife, conspired to lie to the Apostles about the purchase price, holding some back for themselves (Acts 5:1-11). Each one separately lied, and each one dropped dead on the spot. Did this deed really deserve a divine death penalty? In Qumran the penalty for one "who has lied knowingly concerning goods" is exclusion from the "pure food of the Many" for a year and reduction to a quarter of his bread (1Q VI:24).

Some medical specialists support the facticity of the Annanias and Sapphira report in Acts (Howard 2001: 209-210). In cultures that believe certain people have power to heal or to harm, the effective element is often an authoritative command. The intense emotional stress caused by hearing the command can induce acute heart failure. The effect results from cardiogenic shock produced by the sympathetic nervous system over which human beings have no control. Hearing Peter's severe judgment could literally have killed the couple.

Yet perhaps the death should not be interpreted literally. Mediterranean cultural values offer an alternative plausible interpretation. Secrecy, deception, and lying are legitimate and acceptable strategies for preserving one's reputation, one's honor in the Mediterranean world (Pilch 1999: 46–51). Secrecy, deception, and lying simply restrict the public flow of information over a period of time. In this world, no one has a right to know anything. Since a person can trust no one but his or her own family, it is permissible and expected to lie to all except one's own family. One may never lie to the family, although saying what a family member expects to hear is not considered a lie (see Matt 21:28-31 where the son who lied behaved honorably if not obediently). This behavior is true in other cultures as well where a lie prevents offending another person. For instance, explicitly declining an invitation shames the one offering it. So in these cultures, one does not say "no" but "maybe" which everyone understands to mean maybe yes and maybe no.

It may well be that Ananias and Sapphira had to cut ties with their families when they joined the Jesus group (see Luke 12:51-53). Such who joined the Jesus group made it into a surrogate family (Luke 8:19-21), one that replaced their family of origin. We have already noticed how close knit the Jesus group was (Acts 2:44-45; 4:32-37). If one may never lie to one's family, one ought not lie to the surrogate family either. Who would trust those who severed ties with their family of origin and then betrayed their surrogate family? Lying to one's surrogate family is social suicide, since all social activity is rooted in family networks. Such devastating social death would indeed strike great fear in the community and every one else in Mediterranean culture.

For reflection:

1. It is difficult for modern believers to appreciate the importance, indeed legitimacy, of secrecy, deception, and lying in the support and defense of reputation or honor. How would you explain this to such troubled believers?

2. Which interpretation seems more plausible to you, i.e., literally dropped dead or socially cut off because they lied to their family? Why?

ACTS 5:12–42 PUBLIC TEMPLE TOUR: GOD CONTINUES TO ACT IN THE TEMPLE

Acts 5:12-16 Healing

This passage is the third and last of the major summaries in Acts (2:42-47; 4:32-35; 5:11-16). In other words, it generalizes events that have just preceded, hence the theme: "signs and wonders." The Apostles are said to do the same kinds of mighty deeds as those attributed to Peter (v. 12; 3:1-11; 5:1-11). The contradiction in vv. 13 and 14 is only apparent. People hesitated to associate with the Apostles who gathered in Solomon's portico on their own initiative. Recognizing the powers of the Apostles, people realized that it might be best to approach them through an intermediary, a broker. On the other hand, many continued to join the group, or more correctly, the Lord continued to add to their number. The Lord is in charge.

People brought the sick even from towns neighboring Jerusalem so that they might at least be touched by the shadow of Peter as he walked by. This reminds a reader of the power attributed to the hem of Jesus' garment (Luke 8:44) or face cloths and aprons touched by Paul (Acts 19:11-12). However, there is more to be said. In antiquity, the shadow was considered to be a person's or animal's soul, life force, *doppelgänger*, or alter ego. It is possible to harm another person by working violence on his or her shadow. Conversely, it can be a blessing or a curse to touch the shadow of certain people or animals (Van der Horst 1976/7: 204-212).

Contemporary medical anthropologists among others have repeated "all healing is faith healing." A sick person stands a good chance of finding relief and effective healing by trusting the healer, the healer's strategies, and the medications. So powerful is this faith that sometimes placebos are effective. (A placebo is an inert or innocuous substance prescribed more for the psychological satisfaction of a sick person than for its actual effectiveness.) Here in Luke's report, the point is that God continues to act mercifully toward people through the agency of the Apostles, including the mere shadow of Peter.

Acts 5:17-42 Defending

The successes of Peter and the Apostles filled the High Priest and Sadducees with jealousy. They ordered the Apostles to be arrested and imprisoned (vv. 17-28). Though ancient Mediterranean writers distinguished between envy and jealousy, they did not always use the respective Greek words (*phthonos* and *zelos*) with precision (Hagedorn and Neyrey 1998: 19). In general, envy is a feeling of distress at the success of another person, a "bad" thing. Jealousy arises from a concern to defend one's family, property, or reputation against encroachment by others, a "good" thing. The Temple personnel in this passage are described as filled with jealousy (a good thing), but in reality they are really distressed by the success of the Apostles. The broader context makes it clear they are envious (a bad thing). For one, the number of believers in Jesus keeps growing (Acts 5:14), which translates for losses to the Temple group. Second, the reputation of Peter and the Apostles is also growing, which also means that the reputation of the High Priest and Sadducees is diminishing. This culture believes that all goods are limited and already distributed. There is no more where this came from. If one gains, another loses. The increase in followers and reputation for the Apostles signals losses for the Temple personnel.

The response is drastic. The Sanhedrin is convened to put the Apostles on trial for disobeying a prohibition to teach "in that name" (v. 28) and for blaming the High Priest and associates for Jesus' death. The Apostles once again boldly repeat that God raised Jesus, and they prefer to obey God rather than mortals. The decision of the Sanhedrin was to put the Apostles to death.

But then an interesting turn of events occurs. Gamaliel, a Pharisee, intervenes. This is the first mention of Pharisees in Acts, but Luke's audience are already familiar with them from his Gospel. While they were frequently in conflict with Jesus, they often gathered to hear him. Some invited him for dinner (Luke 5:17; 7:26; 11:37; 14:1). Others tipped Jesus off about Herod Antipas' plot to kill him (Luke 13:31). At the end of Jesus' life they disappear from the screen, which is then occupied chiefly by the Sadducees, chief priests, high priest, elders, and scribes (Luke 19:47; 20:1-2, 19, 27-47; 22:1-6, 54-71). And it is this group that now holds the fate of the Apostles in its hands.

Gamaliel is very honorable. He is "respected by all the people" (Acts 5:34) and recognizes that the Apostles also hold similar respect: "The people esteemed them" (Acts 5:13; see 2:47). Ordering the Apostles to be removed from the assembly for a brief while, Gamaliel rehearsed two recent popular reform movements that arose and were checked by the Romans. If this movement is no different from the two he mentions, it, too, will die out. But if it is of God, it would be foolhardy to resist it. In other words, God will ultimately decide. The assembly is persuaded, but they do not dismiss the Apostles without flogging them and ordering them once more "to stop speaking in the name of Jesus" (Acts 5:40). The Apostles, however, rejoiced in their "dishonor" and continued teaching Jesus, the Messiah, in the Temple and at home.

We passed over the imprisonment of the Apostles and their escape in the storyline in order to return to it now (Acts 5:19-20). Some scholars think this story is an abbreviated form of the tradition about Peter reported in Acts 12:6-17 and transferred here. That fuller version of an escape from prison is often described as a conventional literary form, familiar from and similar to other such rescue stories in the propaganda formulated by other political religions. But such literary forms are culturally specific wording patterns that derive from the social system. Genre always derives from the social system because genres are not part of language or the linguistic system. The similarities in the stories are due to the fact that they report a predictable, Mediterranean cultural behavior pattern. Altered states of consciousness serve many functions. Clearly here and in Acts 12 a rescue from prison occurs in a trance experience.

A being from the realm of God (alternate reality), an angel of the Lord opened the prison doors and gave the Apostles a message. Beings from the realm of God (alternate reality) communicate with people in ordinary reality in altered states of consciousness. Physical events effected by beings from alternate reality really do occur in ordinary reality. The holy Spirit, power of the Most High overshadowed Mary, and she became pregnant (Luke 1:35; recall the comments about Peter's "shadow" on p. 50 above). An angel of the Lord opened the doors of the Apostles' prison and led them to freedom (Acts 5:17). There are no specifics about how the Apostles escaped other than that they communicated with an angel very likely in an altered state of consciousness. The anthropologist Dr. Robinette Kennedy (*As the Crow Flies,* vol. 2, #1, Winter 2001) reports a modern episode that sheds some light on this event. She notes that some subjects who in trance take spirit journeys fasten their body in material reality so that it would be waiting for them upon their return. "Supposedly, Houdini could perform genuine feats of magic because of his training in levitation techniques from the same Western Asian shamanic traditions (Siberia and Mongolia), which allowed his spirit to survive while his body withstood remarkable physical trials. When he would return to his body, which he had left in a life-threatening situation, he would find the ropes untied and the locks opened."

Moreover, Rouget (1985: 13–14) offers an observation that confirms that the Apostles were in trance (whether factually so or only in Luke's report):

> Behavioral signs of trance: one can walk on burning coals without being burned, pierce one's own flesh without bleeding, bend swords one would normally be unable to curve, confront dangers without flinching, handle poisonous snakes without being bitten, cure disease, see into the future, embody a divinity, speak a language one has never learned, swoon or die of emotion, be illuminated by the Eternal, enter into contact with the dead, travel in the land of the gods, confront those gods, emit totally unhuman cries, give acrobatic displays beyond one's normal ability, bend backwards to make a perfect arc, compose poems in one's sleep, sing for days and nights on end without a break, dance without difficulty despite being crippled.

Secondly, the Apostles are given a specific instruction: "Go and take your place in the temple area, and tell the people everything about this life" (Acts 5:20). One function of trance experiences is to provide an answer to a question, a solution to a problem, a nudge toward the proper path to take in life at a particular juncture. The Apostles obeyed the messenger early that very morning. They were convinced this was the work of God. "We must obey God rather than men" (Acts 5:29; compare 4:19).

For reflection:

1. Westerners are accustomed to seeking the "scientific" answers as the best answers available. The truly scientific explanation for the Apostles' escape from prison is that it occurred in an alternate state of consciousness. How would you assess alternative explanations: they had help from the inside; it is purely a literary way of expressing an event—religious propaganda; it is a miracle; it never happened?

2. Is there any evidence from "out of the body" experiences that could support this phenomenon?

Chapter 3

Acts 6–12
The Journey beyond Jerusalem
Individual and Communal ASCs

This section (Acts 6–12) is held together by repeated use of the verbs "spread" (Acts 6:7; 12:24), "grow" (Acts 6:1; 9:31), and "increase" (Acts 6:1, 7; 12:24, RSV). People outside the circle of the Twelve begin to play key roles: Stephen (Acts 7), Philip, (Acts 8), Paul (Acts 9). The story moves geographically beyond Jerusalem, though the headquarters remains there (6:1–8:3; 12:1-25). Persecution and conversion become familiar themes in this section. Stephen is stoned to death (6:8–8:1), and James is murdered by Herod's command (12:1-2). Saul at first a persecutor (7:58–8:3; 9:1-2, 21) eventually becomes persecuted himself (9:23-24, 29-30). Conversion is yet another theme that emerges in Acts 8–11: Samaritans and non-Israelites; the Ethiopian eunuch, Saul, and Cornelius embrace Jesus the Messiah and join the group. The conversion events include vivid and dramatic altered states of consciousness experiences that occur in bright daylight.

ACTS 6:1–8:3 STEPHEN THE MARTYR IN JERUSALEM

Acts 6:1-7 Introduction

Stephen is introduced in this section as one of seven men "filled with faith and the holy Spirit" (v. 5). The Australian biblical scholar John N. Collins (1992) offers a very plausible interpretation of this passage considerably different from the popular view. The appropriate cultural context for understanding these verses is that, in general, the people in Palestine spoke Greek, while the Apostles spoke Aramaic. Greek speaking male believers from the house of Israel (Hellenists) complained that their Greek speaking widows were being excluded from the "daily ministry" (preferable to "daily distribution" NAB) by this language disparity. Greek speaking widows could not understand the Aramaic instructions given by the Apostles.

In response, the Twelve did *not* complain that they were being asked to set aside preaching in order to engage in menial work, that is, "To serve at table" (NAB; NRSV) or feed the widows and thereby to "neglect the word of God" (v. 2). Collins proposes as a more plausible translation of Acts 6:2: "It is not right that we [Twelve] should leave aside the public proclamation of the word [in the Temple] to carry out our ministry during mealtimes of the widows."

This cultural world is rigidly divided along gender lines. Even families do not eat together at one table. Men eat with the boys older than the age of puberty, and women eat separately with the girls and all the boys younger than the age of puberty. Thus the idea in this report is not serving meals but rather carrying out this preaching activity in the vicinity of tables, i.e., at home, in private space, where widows have gathered at table, not to eat but to learn. The Apostles as leaders of the group feel they more properly belong in the public forum, in this case, the Temple, where Mediterranean males typically gather to discuss various topics.

The Apostles come up with a solution that pleased and was accepted by the entire community. The community was to select from its midst (1) men [this is the exclusive Greek word that does not include women] of good repute; (2) full of the Spirit (3) and of wisdom. In a word, the community should select men who were capable of preaching. Still, it is important to note that while the community selects them, the Apostles appoint or formally commission them. Deputizing these men for the task of preaching allows the Twelve to continue to perform long prayers of praise and ministry of the word in the Temple. Moreover, these "deacons" were not required to have been with the Lord from his baptism as were the Apostles (see Acts 1:21-22). Thus from the very beginning, the Church controlled the supply of the ministers proposed to them by the community. The men selected each has a Greek name: Stephan, Philip, Prochorus, Nicanor, Timon, Parmenas, and Nicholas. This latter man is from Antioch, hence from the Diaspora and is also a convert to Judaism.

In conclusion, then, according to Luke, ministry involves proclaiming the word to unbelievers (in the Temple) and nurturing the word among believers ("at table" in the home). Ministry, thus, is inextricably linked with purveying the word of God, and those who do it are selected by the community and inducted into their duties by authorities in the Church.

For reflection:

1. Collins' answer to the question in the title of his book *Are All Christians Ministers*? is a resounding "No"! If we take seriously the qualifications for ministry proposed here by the Apostles (men; full of Spirit and of wisdom), what ministries exist in the Church today? Who would be likely candidates?

Acts 6:8–8:3 Stephen, the Martyr

Just before he died, Stephen entered an altered state of consciousness in which he experienced God and Jesus at God's right hand (Acts 7:55-56). Yet the entire report about Stephen prepares the reader for this moment and indeed leads to it. Stephen is one of the seven "reputable men, filled with the Spirit and wisdom" (Acts 6:3), Greek speaking members of the house of Israel, whom the Apostles appointed to tend to the needs of the Greek speaking widows of the house of Israel. Stephen appears first in the list and is described as "a man filled with faith (= loyalty to God) and the holy Spirit (= the power of God, a reward for his loyalty)" (Acts 6:5). In fact, throughout the narrative, he is described in similar terms: "filled with grace (= being pleasing to God) and power (hence, empowered by God)," Stephen "was working great wonders and signs" (Acts 6:8). His opponents "could not withstand the wisdom and the Spirit with which he spoke" (Acts 6:10). Stephen is without doubt a holy man in his culture, someone capable of communicating directly with God and brokering God's favor to other human beings.

Because his opponents could not withstand his wisdom and spirit, that is, because Stephen shamed them, they resorted to a typical Mediterranean strategy for shaming him in return: lying. Shame, like honor, is a public event. Stephen shamed these Greek speaking members of the house of Israel in their synagogues. They seek to shame him before the Sanhedrin. This institution took different forms throughout various times in history, but it would be fair to say that the Sanhedrin among other things was equivalent to a court.

In the ancient Middle East, courts did not always guarantee justice. Whoever took a case to court was considered a loser, because he should have been able to settle before taking this step. But whoever was taken to court could also expect to lose. False witnesses were common (Prov 25:18). It was best to avoid going to court if at all possible (Prov 25:8-10; Matt 5:25-26). Stephen's enemies instigate false witnesses who claim that he blasphemed Moses and God, and that he speaks against the Temple and the Torah. Worse than that, Stephen is charged with claiming that "Jesus the Nazorean will destroy this place and change the customs that Moses handed down to us" (Acts 6:14). Such were their lies. Commentators correctly point out that Luke has drawn an obvious parallel between the false witnesses against Stephen and the false witnesses against Jesus, and at his trial Stephen shares Jesus' fate.

Luke concludes this section by noting that the Sanhedrin "looked intently" (Acts 6:15) at him and saw that his face was "like the face of an angel" (Acts 6:15). Angels in Acts are powerful figures; they should be feared if they are acting against someone (Acts 5:19; 12:7; etc.). Given the importance of Moses in the false charges, it is also plausible that Luke's description of Stephen is a deliberate allusion to Moses' appearance when he came down from his encounter with God on the mountain (Exod 34:29-35; Luke 9:28-36). Anyone looking intently at Stephen should perceive in him a prophet like Moses.

It may be possible to go even further. We have already learned that Stephen is a holy man and a very persuasive speaker. "Looking intently" translates a Greek word that often signals that a person is in trance (Acts 3:4; see above). This is all the more the case when the subject of the verb is a holy man. We have already met one member of the Sanhedrin who might qualify as a holy man, Gamaliel. There could be others. But even if one were to deny this, it is also possible to conclude that Stephen "enchanted" the Sanhedrin by his person, his appearance alone. Even before he begins to speak to this body, his charismatic person has begun working its entrancing effect. His actual message could intensify that effect. Spees (2002) has argued that good storytelling has the ability to induce trance and work therapeutic changes in clinical psychiatric practice.

For reflection:

1. In the cultures of the world that readily experience altered states of consciousness, regular practice improves the ability. People slip in and out of many different levels of awareness each day, often without even noticing. The experience can be triggered or induced by meeting a charismatic person or being enchanted by a captivating speaker. Where might a believer expect this to happen? How might this compare to a person's increased capacity for "mindfulness" in the Buddhist tradition or reflection in the Judaeo-Christian tradition?

2. It is not presumptuous to conclude that people who engage in such activities gradually become better people, more attuned to alternate reality and prepared to relate to it. Indeed, some can enter the trance with minimal preparation time because their life-style is one that is open to that experience. We will notice in subsequent trance reports in Acts, that trance often occurs while a person is or people are praying. The phrases with which Luke describes Philip clearly mark him as such a person: in tune with God, God's spirit, and alternate reality—God's abode. How does Stephen as a holy man serve as a model for modern believers?

In his speech Stephen selects heroes from the tradition, not a few of whom experienced God in an altered state of consciousness. The God of glory appeared to Abraham and spoke with him (Acts 7:2-3). God was with Joseph ("that master dreamer" and interpreter of dreams, Gen 37:19; Acts 7:9). Moses was beautiful before God (Acts 7:20), and in trance he saw and spoke with God appearing in a fire in a bush (Acts 7:30). David found favor in the sight of God (Acts 7:46). Stephen had good models of religious ecstatic trance in the tradition. Altered state of consciousness experience is not alien to this tradition (Goodman 1990: 59).

This longest of the speeches in Acts is a selective presentation and interpretation of key stages in the history of Israel. Stephen does not rebut the charges in Acts 6:13-14. Instead, he directs a few barbed remarks to the Sanhedrin relative to "this land where you now dwell" (Acts 7:4). Stephen is a member of the house of Israel from the Diaspora. Long before the construction of the Temple, Israel's ancestors encountered God in other places, other lands. God identified Mount Sinai to Moses as "holy ground" (Acts 7:33) long before a holy land and holy Temple came into existence. God cannot be constrained as the Temple authorities would wish.

At the conclusion of his speech (Acts 7:51-53), Stephen appeals to "the Most High" (God, Acts 7:48) as the final judge of the charge that he spoke against Moses and God (Acts 6:11). Actually, God is mentioned twelve times in Acts 7:2-44. God does not need a place, a Temple. "The heavens are my throne, / the earth is my footstool" (Acts 7:49 citing Is 66:1-2). This introduced Stephen's final challenge to his priestly judges. He now charges them directly: In magnificent Mediterranean cultural fashion, Stephen eloquently insults his opponents by calling them names: stiff-necked, uncircumcised in heart and ears, Spirit opposers, prophet persecuters and killers, and law breakers. It is no surprise that his speech infuriated them (v. 54).

By grinding their teeth at him (v. 54), the Sanhedrin signals its hostility and intent to harm him (Job 16:9; Ps 35:16; 37:12; 112:10; Lam 2:16). Stephen slips into trance. It may have been induced by his eloquent speech. Musicians and actors readily acknowledge that a good performance can induce trance on stage as well as in the audience. Or it is also possible that sensing his imminent death induces Stephen's trance. He "looks intently" to (gazes or stares at) the sky where he sees God and Jesus standing at God's right hand. This Greek verb ("look intently") has already been identified as a sign of trance when a holy person is the subject. He tells the bystanders what he sees. What does he see? The British scholar J. Duncan M. Derrett noted that the standing Jesus is a broker or mediator, that is, someone presenting a case on behalf of a client. A seated Jesus, the more familiar New Testament image, is one who is exercising power. So Stephen tells them that the risen Jesus is interceding for him with God, assuring his welcome into the realm of God. That, of course, only intensifies their hostility and murderous intent.

As he dies (Acts 7:54–8:3), Stephen commends his spirit to the Lord Jesus, and in imitation of his master prays for forgiveness for his murderers (Luke 23:34, 46). Devout friends (holy men) bury Stephen and grieve for him. Luke briefly introduces Saul as a witness who consented to Stephen's execution (v. 59), then moves the story forward to tell of the persecution that broke out in Jerusalem, scattering all but the Apostles. Paul is a lead player in the persecution.

For reflection:

1. In addition to Abraham, Moses, David, and others mentioned by Stephen in his speech, how many other persons in the Hebrew Bible experienced God in altered states of consciousness? (Hint: think of the prophetic calls, Isaiah 6:1-13; Jeremiah 1; Ezekiel 1:4-28; 8:1-4; 10:1-22; etc.).

2. Even people in our culture which is very skeptical about such experiences sometimes have a trance experience at the moment of death or in a near-death event. A few moments before her death, a woman battling cancer said to her sister: "Franny, those streets really are paved with gold. I know. I've seen them." Are you familiar with any such experiences?

ACTS 8:4-40 PHILIP THE EVANGELIST IN SAMARIA/JUDEA

Acts 8:4-24 Philip, Simon, and the Samaritans

The death of Stephen and the outbreak of persecution forces the believers to move beyond Jerusalem. The next stop on the journey is Samaria, and the person in focus here is Philip, another one of the seven commissioned to teach. But Philip, like Stephen, does not restrict himself to teaching Hellenist widows, the context in which these men were appointed to ministry. They took their ministry beyond that. Stephen addressed Temple personnel. Philip, from Caesarea Maritima (Acts 21:8), is the first one in Acts to bear witness beyond Jerusalem.

Philip's success in Samaria is nothing short of astounding. These ancient enemies of Israel (2 Kgs 17:20ff.; Ezra 4:1-5; Sir 50:25-26) who refused to receive Jesus and his message (Luke 9:51-54) now enthusiastically respond to Philip's preaching about Jesus, the Messiah, and convert! Luke's reports that Peter and John had to come and impart the Spirit that they did not receive with their baptism in the name of Jesus (Acts 8:14-17) probably does not represent a historical fact. It is more plausibly an attempt by Luke to subordinate Samaritan believers in Jesus, the Messiah, to Jerusalem authorities lest at the very beginning there should be two parallel Jesus movements: Judean and Samaritan. The Spirit works only in those groups who retain communion with the "witness to his resurrection" (Act 1:22).

Luke paints an interesting contrast between Philip and Simon, a magician (Acts 8:4-24). Philip worked mighty deeds, expelled demons, and healed the paralyzed and lame but mainly preached Jesus, the Messiah. Simon was in Samaria long before Philip's arrival and had amazed the Samaritans with his magic. He claimed to be the Great Power of God incarnate (Acts 8:9-11). Rather than becoming jealous of Philip, Simon converts, is baptized, and becomes Philip's constant companion.

What does magic mean? In general, it is a form of communication with beings in alternate reality. The strategy of magic is to use ritual actions or formulaic recitations to force these beings to work a desired impact on ordinary reality. Ancient magic is about control. It has nothing in common with the contemporary understanding of magic. Although Simon's (bad) reputation grew and developed in various sources (Acts of Peter, Justine Martyr, Irenaeus, et al.), the information in these verses is too meager to conclude anything very definitively. At most, it is clear that Simon was a contemporary of the Apostles, and he was a syncretist enjoying great popularity in Samaria.

Luke sketches a difference between Philip and Simon. Philip turns attention to God who is the real healer; Simon uses his power to bedazzle the people rather than to benefit them, hoping to keep their attention focused on him. Despite his conversion, Simon seems too narrowly focused on what he "saw," namely, "signs and mighty deeds" by Philip (Acts 8:13), and the Apostles conferring the Spirit by laying hands on the Samaritans (Acts 8:18). He is still interested in bedazzling the people rather than brokering grace to them. When Simon offers to buy the kind of power Peter has in the laying on of hands (origin of the word "simony"), he seriously challenges (insults) Peter who rightly rebukes him. God's gifts can't be bought (Acts 8:20).

In the Mediterranean world, all goods are viewed as finite in quantity and already distributed. Peter and John clearly have one of these goods, an ability to impart the Spirit to others. By offering to buy this gift for himself, Simon is willing to deprive them not only of some power but also of the reputation or honor this gift brings in its wake. It is also a strategy by Simon to regain some of the honor he has lost with the advent of Philip, Peter, and John to Samaria. This is the reason for Peter's stinging rebuke and challenge that Simon repent and pray for forgiveness (Acts 8:20-23). Simon gets the message. He is so chastened and humiliated that he dare not pray on his own initiative. Instead, he asks Peter and John as privileged mediators to pray for him to the Lord. We do not know for certain what happened to Simon except that subsequent Jesus group tradition labeled him "Magus" (magician). The movement associated with his name was influenced by the Jesus group and developed into a distinct form of Gnosticism. By the time of Origen (A.D. 186–253) the Simon movement or form of Gnosticism was dying out.

For reflection:

1. Even in the contemporary technologically proficient world, human experience often points out that many dimensions of life lie beyond human control. Those who believe that God has control turn to God in prayer. How does this prayer differ from the request of Simon the magician?

2. Is there a risk that some Christians might begin to view traditional formulaic recitations as a form of magic, as a rite that can force beings in the realm of God or alternate reality (God, the saints, deceased ancestors) to grant the wishes of petitioners? How can this risk be avoided? What is the contemporary understanding of "magic"? Does that help or hinder understanding of antiquity?

Acts 8:25-40 The Ethiopian Eunuch and the Ends of the Earth

Philip and the others return to Jerusalem, but an angel of the Lord tells Philip to continue on the road south from Jerusalem to Gaza (v. 26). It is possible and indeed preferable to translate the Greek word rendered "south" as "noon, or midday" (as it is regularly in the Septuagint; see also Acts 22:6, the only other place this word occurs in Acts). But no one travels in the Middle East at this time of day (see Sir 43:3)! What does this mean? Perhaps Luke signals to the reader that something extraordinary is going to happen, a significant "enlightenment" is about to take place. Later in Luke's story, Peter falls into trance at noon (Acts 10:10) as does Paul (Acts 22:6). For Luke, then, the word is not a geographical direction but rather an important time indicator.

Who is this angel of the Lord? Scholars recognize that the Israelites evolved their way of referring to God from first using the actual divine name (YHWH), then substituting "Lord" in order not to pronounce that name, and eventually adopting the phrase "angel of the Lord" to refer to God. By New Testament times, this "angel of the Lord" concept was personalized as one of God's messengers. It could be an angel (e.g., Acts 5:19) or the Spirit (Acts 8:29, 39; 10:19; 11:12; 13:2).

However it is interpreted in this passage, Luke's use of the phrase tells us that Philip was inspired or instructed by God on a course of action. Did this occur in an altered state of consciousness? It is plausible that as he journeyed, Philip entered into a trance state much the same as contemporary drivers of automobiles sometimes do. Practically everyone who drives a car has experienced arriving at a destination and presumably observing speed limits, signal lights and the rest, without actually remembering the journey. Sometimes called "road trance," this illustrates what Milton Erickson has identified as "the common everyday trance." In this case, Philip's "common everyday trance" directs him to continue his journey.

Along the road, Philip encounters an Ethiopian minister of the Candace, queen of the Ethiopians, on his way back from Jerusalem to Ethiopia, reading the prophet Isaiah. It is important to remember than in antiquity all reading involved moving the lips and speaking the words out loud. Silent reading without moving the lips is a much later discovery in human history. Again, Philip is inspired by the Spirit to catch up with the man's chariot. When he hears the man reading Isaiah, Philip asks if he understands. The man asks for help, suggesting he may not have found adequate help in Jerusalem in understanding the Scripture. (Such a refusal from knowledgeable interpreters in Jerusalem might have been provoked by the Mosaic critique of eunuchs, Deut 23:2.) Philip interprets the passage (Isa 53:7ff) for him and continues to tell him the good news about Jesus. Coming upon some water (in the desert!?!), the minister requests baptism, and Philip obliges him. The "Spirit of the Lord" immediately removed Philip from this place to Azotus, where he preached the Gospel to all towns until he reached Caesarea. The eunuch continues his homeward journey rejoicing.

In the ancient world, Ethiopians were viewed as people of great piety and beauty. In the *Iliad* (1.423-34), Homer speaks of "blameless Ethiopians." Herodotus praised these "burnt-skinned" Ethiopians by calling them the tallest and most handsome of all humankind (*History* 3.20). Diodorus of Sicily claimed that "it is generally held that the sacrifices practiced among the Ethiopians are those which are most pleasing to heaven" (3.3.1). Such an eminently worthy "god-fearer" (for this is what he seems to be) was apparently spurned as an outcast in Jerusalem but evangelized and baptized by Philip, likely also considered an outcast (as a follower of Jesus) by Jerusalem authorities. Ethiopia, located due south of Egypt, was famous in Greco-Roman traditions as the most distant outpost of the known world (*Odyssey* 1.22-24; Strabo, *Geography*, 17.2.1-3). The clear significance of this story for Luke is that Philip has made the first boundary breaking move in this eunuch to bringing the good news of Jesus "to the ends of the earth" (Acts 1:8).

How are we to understand Philip's sudden disappearance, and the eunuch's apparent lack of surprise or wonder at this experience? In trance, people sometimes make journeys either to one or another dimension of alternate reality such as the underworld, or to the sky, or elsewhere (Gore 1995: 163–208; Goodman 1990: 71–78). Paul briefly mentions his trip to "the third heaven," "paradise" (2 Cor 12:2, 4). Ezekiel took a trip from Babylon to Jerusalem (Ezek 8:3).

Here in Acts we can conclude that Philip was in trance during most if not all of this experience, from the moment he was inspired to continue beyond Jerusalem until the moment he found himself in Azotus. Material reality (in which we live) and alternate reality (in which God, our ancestors, and spirits live) sometimes overlap. We have already learned about the entry point, the crack, or opening between ordinary and alternate reality (see pp. 18–19 above; Acts 1). In actuality, a person in trance can slip into, out of, and back into trance (Goodman 2001: 429). Peter saw Jesus walking on the Sea, and Peter walked successfully on the Sea toward Jesus in trance (Matt 14:29). This takes place in alternate reality. When Peter left the trance ("sees the wind . . . was afraid" [RSV]), he understandably began to sink because he had returned to ordinary reality.

Similarly in this story, the eunuch may also have been in trance, in alternate reality, with Philip. After the eunuch's baptism, Philip was "snatched . . . away" by the Spirit of the Lord. The verb translated "snatched away" typically appears in reports of sky journeys (2 Cor 12:2, 4; 1 Thess 4:17; Rev 12:5; 2 Kgs 2:16). When Philip suddenly disappeared (v. 39), the trance ended for the eunuch. He was now satisfied that he had learned the interpretation of the puzzling passage in Isaiah. Having accepted baptism, he continued his journey in material reality with great joy. Meanwhile, presumably Philip's trance continued as he journeyed to Azotus on the seacoast just north of Ascalon.

For reflection:

1. Have you ever thought about how God communicates with human beings? In this story, we read about the angel of the Lord. In another part of Scripture, we read about vision (1 Sam 3:1). How else do the Scriptures tell us that God communicates with human beings? How does God communicate with you (and you with God)?

2. John the astral prophet tells us in Revelation that in trance (Rev 1:10) he took journeys to the sky that gave him insight into God's will (Rev 4:1-2; 17:3; 21:10). In our story, Philip takes a journey in trance to Azotus. Have you ever made a journey in trance? Do you know anyone who made a journey in an altered state of consciousness?

ACTS 9:1-31 SAUL—PERSECUTION IN DAMASCUS AND JERUSALEM

Luke tells the story of Paul's experience on the way to Damascus three times in Acts (9:1-9; 22:3-21; 26:9-18). Nowhere in his letters does Paul recount the details that Luke does. In Galatians (1: 16), Paul simply states that he came to know and understand Jesus, the Messiah, in a revelation that would be a trance experience, an altered state of consciousness experience. He seems reluctant to speak of his trance experiences (see 2 Cor 12). Scholars are not agreed whether Luke's account is factual, interpreted fact, or fictional. Some medical scientists agree that Paul did encounter the risen Jesus in a trance experience, but not as Luke reports it. In fact, they attribute Paul's later visions to post-traumatic epilepsy caused by his many beatings and stoning (2 Cor 11:24-25; Howard 2001: 250–51). In this book, we interpret the experiences as authentic altered states of consciousness events, even though they are interpreted by Luke. Because this story is told three times with more detail than other experiences, we devote more time to it.

Acts 9:1-22 The persecutor becomes proclaimer

Acts 9:1-9 On the way to Damascus

This event has traditionally been called the "conversion of Paul." Actually, that is one interpretation of the report. It is more appropriate to name this event "the call of Paul by God to a special function." In fact, a more social-scientific view than "call" would be "recruitment" (see Duling 2001: 132–175). It is also important to notice that Paul does not receive a new name in this event or anywhere in Acts for that matter. Saul begins to be called Paul in Acts 13:9: "Saul, also known as Paul." That translation is significant. In the Hellenistic period, members of the house of Israel had two names: a Semitic one (Saul, which means "asked of God"), and a Greek or Roman name (Paul is the Greek form of a well-known Roman cognomen).

From the viewpoint of cultural anthropology and cognitive neuroscience, this is a report of Paul's altered state of consciousness in which he encounters the risen Jesus. Insights about ecstatic trance or altered states of consciousness from these scientific disciplines help to explain what the basic event might have been and why Luke could interpret it as he did.

To begin with, in his letters Paul deliberately links his experience to the Easter experiences of the other Apostles: "Last of all, as to one born abnormally, he appeared to me" (or "was seen by me"; 1 Cor 15:5-9). Scholars agree that while Luke is careful to distinguish Paul from the other Apostles by designating him as a great envoy to non-believers (Acts 1:21-22), Paul repeatedly insists that he is indeed an apostle (e.g., Gal 1:1). This, however, is not a concern here. We are concerned rather with the pivotal experience in Paul's life that gave Paul unswerving confidence in his status and mission.

Paul's ecstatic trance was plausibly induced by one or both of two causes: travel and intense concentration. Modern travelers are familiar with road trance. Hypnotized by the highway or the boredom of the trip, a modern traveler often arrives safe at a destination to which she or he was driving without explicitly remembering the route, the traffic lights, the turns, etc. We already suggested that this occurred to Philip when he met the Ethiopian eunuch. Research indicates that human beings shift between different levels of consciousness many times during a day, even in the company of others. Students attending a class lecture or scholars participating in a seminar or conference can attest to this experience, no matter how small and intimate the group. That Paul is traveling with companions would therefore not rule out the possibility of his falling into ecstatic trance.

The second and more likely element that induced Paul's trance was intense concentration. Neuroscientists call this a trance induced "from the top down" (d'Aquili and Newberg 1999: 23–27, 99–102; see Acts 3:1-10). What they mean is that certain activities that begin in the cortex of the brain then move down into the autonomic nervous system and contribute to altering a person's level of consciousness. Meditation or any other form of intense concentration is a common strategy for inducing this kind of trance. It is manifest in an extraordinary state of relaxation. The meditation can be positive, that is, the meditator can focus on one idea to the exclusion of all others, or it can be negative, that is, the meditator can deliberately attempt to remove all ideas from consciousness. Meditation produces a hyper-quiescent state, an ecstatic trance experience of longer duration than one caused from the "bottom up" by overstimulating the nervous system.

On his journey, Paul was intensely focused on Jesus group members because they were dishonoring (shaming) the God of Israel, at least according to his Pharisee perspectives. Jesus must surely have been a fraudulent and deceptive teacher, a "holy man" of dubious character. After witnessing and approving the murder of Stephen (Acts 8:1), Paul doggedly sought out believers to have them imprisoned (Acts 8:3). Along the way to Damascus, he was "still breathing murderous threats against the disciples of the Lord" (Acts 9:1), seeking to arrest and bring them to Jerusalem in chains. Such intense focus on one idea greatly contributed to inducing Paul's altered state of consciousness.

Other neuropsychological scientists have identified and described three overlapping stages of ecstatic trance (Siegel 1977; for application to shamanic trance, see Dowson 1992: 29–65; Clottes and Lewis-Williams 1996: 16–19). Clottes and Lewis-Williams (1996: 19) underscore the fact that these three stages are universal and hard-wired, as it were, into the human nervous system. It is not important for a visionary to pass through all three stages, but the three stages seem to cover the range of possible experience. Luke's account of Paul's experience reflects two of the stages. In the first, or lightest stage of trance, visionaries see various geometric forms: dots, zigzags resembling lightning strikes, lines or sticks that may be parallel, crossed, vertical, horizontal, and the like. One also sees bright colors that can flicker, pulsate, or blend with one another. To see pale white is a fairly good indicator one is in trance. To see only black or dark could mean one has not yet entered trance or that one has left it. As already noted above (p. 20), these colors relate to different levels of neurological activity and different brain wave activity. Some societies give meanings to these geometric forms, while others do not. For example, the South American Tukano interpret brilliant dots as the Milky Way, the goal of their sky journeys (Reichel-Dolmatoff 1978). To see them would indicate to the visionary that she or he has arrived at the journey's goal. However, many meanings are possible and do exist.

The bright light from heaven (Acts 9:3; 22:6), even brighter than the sun (26:13), that Paul saw is typical of stage one of an ecstatic trance. That he does not report seeing geometric forms is not significant. Either Paul did not experience them, or never referred to this element, or the tradition or Luke omitted it. In the Israelite tradition, light is the manifestation of God's honor or glory (Isa 60:1; 62:1; Luke 2:9), that is, God's very self. The light takes the form of a cloud (Exod 24:15ff) or fire (Deut 5:24) flashing brightly (Ezek 1:4, 27-28; 10:4). From a neurological perspective, the bright color signals a shift in consciousness (Goodman 1973: 100). From an ideological (theological, personal meaning) perspective, Paul, the Pharisee, familiar with light in the Israelite tradition would be aware that he had entered alternate reality or that some being from alternate reality, the realm of God, might be initiating communication with him.

In the second stage, the visionary attempts to make sense of the geometric forms by imagining or illusioning them into significant objects. Visionaries select objects of personal, religious, emotional, or still other significance. Thus, the bright light or white color seen by some visionaries in Acts would certainly be associated with the realm of God. As already noted, YHWH's glory is always described as bright light. Since Jesus and angels are just some of the beings in the realm of God, an Israelite visionary would certainly use these subjects to try to imagine what he or she is seeing. Visions are never clear like a photograph. They are always vague and fuzzy. Sometimes the visionary's emotional state influences the interpretation. If a person is thirsty, the object might become a cup of water; if the person is frightened, the object could become a weapon. Peter's emotional state (hunger) occasioned the content of his vision reported in Acts 10 and later its interpretation.

In Luke's account, after falling to the ground Paul does not report seeing any being. He saw rather a flash of light. Next, he heard a voice asking him a question: "Saul, Saul, why are you persecuting me?" (Acts 9:4; 22:7; 26:14). Ecstatic trance experiences often reflect and include recent personal experiences (Goldman 1999). Paul was persecuting the disciples of the Lord. Which one is speaking to him? "Who are you, sir? . . . I am Jesus" (Acts 9:5; 22:8; 26:15).

Paul, the Pharisee, would associate light with the realm of God. In stage two, he seeks to impose meaning on the experience. He hears a voice from that realm. Paul was familiar with the realm of God as it relates to "this world." Paul knew that holy men abide with God and other beings in the realm of God

(Pilch 1998a). It is important to acknowledge that people like Paul (e.g., fellow Israelites) who believe in this alternate reality, the realm of God, also know that beings from there can readily visit and intervene in the life and consciousness of human beings in culturally "normal" or ordinary reality (e.g., Luke 2:26-38). Indeed, beings from alternate reality are most likely to visit those who are familiar with them rather than those completely unfamiliar with them. So when Paul learns the identity of the one appearing to him in trance, many things fall instantly into place. This Jesus (of Nazareth) who died a shameful death now comes from alternate reality (in Israelite tradition, the realm of God) to speak with a person who has hated him. This Jesus must most certainly be pleasing to God, acceptable to God, or he wouldn't be with God in the realm of God. Paul immediately perceived the error of his behavior as a persecutor. He can halt the trance, perhaps deny it, or accept its message and respond accordingly. He allows it to continue. This is God's doing. It is clear from Paul's letters that he recognized that God was instrumental in his having these ecstatic trance experiences. "But when he who had set me apart before I was born . . . was pleased to reveal his Son to me. . ." (Gal 1:15-16, RSV). God took the initiative.

The third stage, deep trance, is ordinarily reached through a tunnel, a vortex, a narrow passageway of some sort between culturally "normal" reality and alternate reality. Sometimes visionaries see a lattice along the sides of the passageway. This appears to be what becomes of the geometric imagery from stage one. Visionaries may begin to see animals, people, or other objects in the lattices. At the end of the passageway the visionary arrives in a bright place (or sometimes a place of subdued light). Sometimes this world seems bizarre, and in this stage visionaries can journey, fly like birds, or even change (metamorphose) into birds or animals or other beings. This, however, is only a first impression. When the trance experience is ended, the visionary gives unusual experiences an interpretation that makes good sense. This is often facilitated by longer reflection, further analysis, or discussion with others, especially if the trance was experienced in a group or communal setting. Luke's three reports do not seem to reveal a third stage in Paul's trance experience. But Paul is said to gain understanding through an interpretation from Ananias.

Let us, however, return to stage two, the dialogue with Jesus. Anthropologists observe that the content of trance experiences is vacuous (Goodman 1990: 17; compare Goodman 2001.9; see p. 4 above). They come without a sound-track (Pilch 1993: 240). It is the visionary who supplies the sound track. Paul clearly hears someone speaking to him, and Paul answers. In the first account, those with him heard the voice but saw no one (Acts 9:7). The "voice" could have been a sound culturally interpreted as communication coming from the sky, from alternate reality (for an example, see John 12:28-30). In the second account, they see the light but do not hear the voice (Acts 22:9). In both accounts, Paul's companions knew that he was in trance (saw the light or heard the voice), but they themselves were not experiencing trance as for instance, Peter, James, and John were at the time of Jesus' transfiguration (Mark 9:2-8 and parallels; see Pilch 1994). In other words, this is not a group trance.

The dialogue in all three accounts appears with very little variation. Lohfink (1976) has analyzed and identified it as a "dialogue with apparition" literary form. It has a tri-partite structure:

A1	Introductory formula	. . . saying to him	Acts 9:4; 22:7; 26:14
A2	double vocative	"Saul, Saul!	
A3	question of Christ	Why are you persecuting me?"	
B1	Introductory formula	But he answered/I said	Acts 9:5; 22:8; 26:15
B2	question of Paul	"Who are you, sir?"	
C1	Introductory formula	The reply came . . .	Acts 9:5: 22:8; 26:15

C2	Self-presentation of Christ	"I am Jesus, whom you are persecuting. . . ."	
C3	Mission	"But rise . . ."	(cf. Acts 9:15; 22:14); 26:16

Felicitas Goodman has identified four elements in the cultural patterning of a trance experience: (1) the one experiencing the vision is initially frightened and (2) does not recognize the figure. (3) The figure in the vision offers calming assurance (e.g., "fear not") and (4) identifies self (e.g., "It is I. . ."; see Pilch 1993; also for calming assurance in Scipio's dream, see Cicero, *The Republic* VI: 10). In the accounts of Paul's experience, there is no indication of fright, thus no need for a statement of calming assurance from the one appearing. He hasn't seen anyone; he has only heard a voice. The cultural patterning identified by Goodman is inclusive, but all elements do not have to occur in each experience. It is not surprising, therefore, that Lohfink (1976) identifies a "shorter version" of this literary form in which the self-presentation is lacking. Thus, God communicates with Ananias, and Ananias recognizes God immediately (Acts 9:10-11). Cornelius sees an angel of God coming to him and is in terror. Since Cornelius recognized his visitor from alternate reality, the realm of God, there was no need of self-identification (Acts 10:33-5; for other examples see Genesis 22:1-2 and 1 Samuel 3:4-15).

Lohfink's identification of this literary form and its variations surfaces a common question. Is this literary form nothing more than a literary device commonly used in the literature to talk about an encounter with God, an angel, or other such beings? The form appears in the Septuagint and is already stable and fixed by the first century A.D. Or does the literary form embellish a very simple experience? In personal e-mail communication, Prof. Bruce Malina pointed out that all of these text-segments report a predictable, Mediterannean *cultural behavioral pattern*. Since trance experiences are quite common ("normal") in the Circum-Mediterranean world (Goodman

1990: 59), the culture prescribes the appropriate behavior for the visionary. Recall the observation of Lewis-Williams (1996: 12) that all people have to cope with different states of consciousness in one way or another.

Culture offers one way of coping by prescribing predictable behavioral patterns, and Goodman has identified four elements that may be found in the pattern. The writing patterns that Lohfink and other form-critics identify in literature are, in Malina's words, "culturally specific wording patterns that derive from the social system. Genre always derives from the social system since genres are not part of language or the linguistic system." Since the social system also specifies the behavioral pattern by which altered states are experienced and interpreted, it is quite plausible that visionaries did behave in just the way the literary pattern reports.

Lohfink correctly cautions that the interpreter cannot consider the dialogues in these three reports as a factual, word-for-word report. He describes them rather as facts-with-interpretation, and claims that it is impossible to date and determine where the facts end and the interpretation begins. Indeed, the meanings given by the visionary to the experiences in each of these stages is culture specific. To quote Clottes and Lewis-Williams (1996: 19) with adaptation, "At least in some measure, people see in visions [they use the word "hallucinate" but not in a pathological sense] what they expect to see [hallucinate]." Once again, cognitive neuroscience helps to gain an even clearer understanding of Luke's reports about Paul's call. Specialists identify two distinct neuroanatomical and neurophysiological mechanisms in the brain (d'Aquili and Newberg 1999: 149-150). The first, the causal operator, perceives and/or imposes causal sequences in the organization of reality. It strives to impose control and order over reality. In other words, this mechanism in the brain always constructs fact-with-interpretation. The second mechanism, the holistic operator, involves the potential for developing and experiencing altered states of consciousness. ASC experiences are not linear but rather holistic. The experiences provide glimpses into the spirit world (scientists sometimes call spirits "personalized power sources") that can be and sometimes are generated or at least perceived by the causal operator.

Scientists also observe that the continuity of consciousness is an illusion (Rossi 1986: 111). The human brain does not store information "whole" but rather in "parts" along a network of nodes. Creative insights occur when the nodes are linked in a pattern different from the ordinary one. While this information can help us understand how Paul came to his new understanding of Jesus in God's plan, we must not forget that God and Jesus wanted it to occur. Why at this time and in this way, we may never know. But without Jesus' will to encounter Paul, the insight might not have occurred at all, or if it did, Paul might have ignored or discarded it as he well might have on previous occasions.

When the trance ends, Paul sees nothing. He apparently has suffered a temporary loss of sight (three days). This is not a common occurrence in trance, but each person's trance experience is distinctive. One always trusts and believes what the visionary reports. And Paul undertakes sensory deprivation (neither ate nor drank) for three days which helps to explain his subsequent trances (Acts 9:12). Fasting is a traditional and very familiar technique for preparing the body to experience the neurological changes that facilitate the inducement of trance. All that Paul has learned at this point is that he should go into Damascus where he will be further instructed.

For reflection:

1. To understand God's call in the way it came, Paul had to know his tradition (Israelite) and culture (Mediterranean) very well (meaning of light, recognizing voice of God, etc.). Where could a modern believer learn this tradition?

2. Interpreting God's call is even more challenging. What prepared Paul the Pharisee for this task? (Hint: Who is a Pharisee?).

3. In 1990, the esteemed biblical scholar Fr. Raymond Brown wrote: ". . . to read the Bible with appropriate comprehension, people's biblical education should be proportionate to his general education; then they can deal with issues that arise from that general education" (*New Jerome Biblical Commentary* 71: 17). Understanding and interpretation depend very much upon one's educational level. When one reads information that differs from what one knows or thinks one knows, one is faced with a challenge. One can reject the new information out of hand, or suspend judgment while pursuing the new insight. How does one incorporate new insights into understanding trance experiences?

4. Paul's experience takes place between Jerusalem (his point of departure) and Damascus (his destination). He is ironically on the road or the "way" (see Acts 9:2). From the perspective of ritual, Paul is in a "liminal" or "threshold" state. He is no longer a persecutor but not yet a disciple or evangelizer. Changes in human life often occur in such liminal situations. For example, engagement is a liminal state between the single state and the married state. The novitiate is a liminal state between secular and religious life. In many cultures, trance often occurs and proves √ very helpful in such situations. Have you ever experienced such liminal situations that eventually resulted in a change of status?

Acts 9:10-19   *The house on Straight Street:*
Ananias sees the Lord in a vision (ASC)

We meet new characters in this segment: Judas and Ananias. They replace apostate characters with the same names who appeared earlier in Acts (1:16-20; 5:1-6). Ananias, about whom we know no more than that he is a disciple (9:10), sees the Lord in a vision. Ananias is not frightened but seems rather to immediately recognize the Lord. When addressed, he replied, "Here I am, Lord." The Lord instructs him to find Saul, and then the Lord tells him of Saul's vision in which Saul saw a certain Ananias restore his sight by the laying on of hands.

Literally, the text says, "The Lord said (to Ananias) in a vision" (v. 10). If visions don't have a soundtrack other than what the visionary supplies, where did Ananias learn about a person named Saul? Quite likely the gossip network already spread the word of Paul's journey to Damascus and its punishing purpose. How would Ananias know that Saul was in Judas' house? While we don't know the size of the community of believers in Damascus, it was quite likely small enough in size that its members knew each other well. They would also know everyone's status and abilities. Judas may have been one of those who would be able to host a visitor. Perhaps it was his task in the community.

In any case, Luke reports two visions (one by Saul and one by Ananias) that are related. This is similar to the transfiguration in which Jesus had a vision (the content of which is not reported) and the three apostles saw Jesus' appearance changed and him conversing with Moses and Elijah (Luke 9:28-36). Such "double" related visions are known in antiquity (see Pilch 1995: 51). An ancient translator of a book of Asclepian healings became ill during his work and sought help from the healing god. His mother was at his bedside. While he slept, she slipped into a waking dream (an altered state of awareness) and saw the god Asclepius heal her son. When she regained ordinary awareness, she woke him to tell her dream, but he told her everything before she said a word (P. Oxy. XI. 1381.91ff = Testimony 331).

Ananias' objection might reveal Luke's sense of humor. Conversing with the risen Jesus, Ananias unthinkingly tells him of Paul's malicious intent, as if Jesus had not known it. Jesus informs Ananias that Saul is "a chosen instrument of mine" (Acts 9:15). It is important to keep in mind that encounters with beings in alternate reality depend on the willingness of those beings to meet visitors from ordinary reality. Luke makes it clear in this episode that the risen Jesus is active in alternate reality with an impact on ordinary reality relative to Saul and Ananias in this episode. The risen Jesus has already informed Paul in trance (while praying!) from whom (Ananias) and how (laying on of hands) he will regain his sight. As for Ananias, the risen Jesus informs him of his plans for Saul: he is to become a chosen instrument of evangelization.

Ananias follows these instructions. His greeting to Paul whom he has never met before is noteworthy: "Saul, my brother" (v. 17). Saul is not yet baptized, nor is he yet a member of the community, but he has encountered and communicated with the risen Jesus as has Ananias. It is this encounter with Jesus in alternate reality that bonds the two men together like brothers. Ananias tells him that. The same Jesus you met also visited me with instructions about you. Immediately Saul regains his sight, is baptized, then eats to regain the strength lost through fasting.

As noted earlier, blindness or loss of sight does not usually accompany an altered state of consciousness experience. Luke's description of Paul's experience contains three significant elements that might be considered factual. There was a bright light (Acts 9:8; 22:11; 26:13). The loss of sight was not permanent. It lasted only three days (Acts 9:9). Restoration of sight seemed to result from desquamation of the cornea ("things like scales fell from his eyes" Acts 9:18). One plausible medical explanation is that Saul suffered a lightning stroke injury. This could entail burns to the cornea, perhaps even the retina. A possible long-term effect is the formation of cataracts (Howard 2001: 253–255). It is difficult to know what role the laying on of hands played in this episode other than that it is associated both with healing and with communication of the spirit. Howard thinks it may have effected a desquamation of the cornea, a sloughing off of the "scabs" from the burns.

For reflection:

1. How would you integrate the insight of Howard in the paragraph immediately above with what has been developed in this section? Is there a contradiction? If so, how would you

resolve it? The larger question is how do medical hypotheses relate to cultural anthropological insights?

2. The Greek word for vision literally means something one can see, whether a person is asleep or awake. Philologists and anthropologists distinguish between a waking vision and a sleeping vision (dream), but both can serve as a vehicle of communication between beings in alternate and ordinary reality. The Lord speaks to Ananias in a waking vision, and later to Paul in a "night vision" (dream; cf. Acts 19:6). If you have had waking visions or "night visions," have you paid sufficient attention to them? Could these be an opportunity for an encounter with God or the risen Lord or others in the realm of God?

Acts 9:19-22 The synagogue in Damascus

After his recovery, Saul began forthwith to preach in the synagogues that Jesus is the Son of God and to prove that he is the Messiah. His audience was understandably confused and astounded. Both claims would confuse fellow Israelites, but the fact that he who came to arrest believers now has become one himself is astounding. The change however is not inexplicable. One result of such ASC experiences is a reorganization of personality structure or a realignment of the individual toward his or her world. Indeed, his realignment to his world is so dramatic, many did not believe him or trust him (see Acts 9:21-25). The report in Acts 22:14 is similar. Ananias explained that the purpose of Paul's ASC experience was to learn God's will, to see Jesus, and to become a witness on his behalf to all people. In the final report, Acts 26:16 (RSV), Paul learned directly from Jesus that he is appointed by him to bear witness "to the things in which you have seen me and to those in which I will appear to you." Of particular interest in verse 16 is the notice that Paul will obtain further instruction from Jesus in other ecstatic trance experiences, which of course Acts bears out (see 16:6-10; 18:9-10; 22:17-21; 23:11).

For reflection:

1. Have you ever had an experience that profoundly changed your life, your personality, your relationship to the world, and the like? What was the nature of the experience? Was it a dream? A vision? Did you see the hand or activity of God in that experience?

Acts 9:23-31 The persecutor becomes the persecuted

The pattern of reaction to Jesus replays itself in the life of his Apostles. Audiences were invariably divided. Some believed and accepted Jesus, others rejected and sought to kill him. The Israelites who were confounded by Saul eventually conspired to kill him. Saul's disciples helped him escape. The reference to disciples is interesting. Has the new convert already made disciples? That would be quite a tribute to his preaching!

In Jerusalem, Saul fares no better. The disciples still fear him until Barnabas acts as a patron for Saul and convinces them of Saul's genuineness. It is noteworthy that Barnabas does not seem to have received any information about Saul in a trance experience as did Ananias. Taking Saul at his word, Barnabas typifies people of this culture. No one denied the visions. They might debate the content or the vision's significance, but they accept the reality of the vision. Barnabas, already a disciple, accepts and reports Saul's experience as he heard it, no doubt personally from Saul. The Hellenists, however, tried to kill him, so the brothers helped him escape to Tarsus.

Acts 9:32–11:18 Peter in Sharon and Caesarea

In this part of his story, Luke presents Peter as complementing the ministry of Philip (8:14-25) in the cities of Lydda (9:32-35) and Joppa (9:36-43) where Philip seems to have previously established believing communities. But in Caesarea, the end of Philip's journey, Peter meets with prospective disciples like

Cornelius and the household. Peter is thus presented as a founder of communities in his own right, not just a developer of those founded by others.

Acts 9:32-43 Peter heals sick people

Scholars point to a similarity between the healing activity of Peter and that of Jesus in these stories of the paralytic Aeneas and the deceased Tabitha/Dorcas. Why should the disciple not imitate the master? Aeneas (Acts 9:32-35) was paralyzed for eight years. Peter insists it is not he, but Jesus who heals. Jesus is the patron. Peter is but Jesus' broker. "Jesus Christ heals you. Get up and make your bed" (v. 34). A currently popular medical explanation of this event is that this paralyzed man (as likely all the paralytics in the New Testament) were suffering from a psychological conversion disorder. Eight years earlier, it is very plausible that Aeneas confronted a reality he couldn't handle. Some experience was too much for him to bear, so hysterical paralysis helped him escape from that reality or experience. This interpretation is proposed by contemporary psychiatry. Peter's command is an abreactive technique perhaps learned from Jesus. To phrase it otherwise, Peter's technique causes an abreaction, which is a paralyzed person's expression and emotional release of unconscious material such as a repressed idea or emotion, especially in the presence of a healer. Peter's abreactive technique is effective (Howard 2001: 205–06). Aeneas got up immediately, which means his paralysis left him. All the inhabitants who recognized the healing "turn[ed] to the Lord" (v. 35).

At Joppa, Peter restored a female disciple to life. Her double name, Tabitha (Aramaic) and Dorcas (Greek, both meaning Gazelle) are typical in this environment. The case is similar to Saul/Paul. She is clearly an important person in the community. A woman of independent means, she gave alms and tended to the needs of widows by supplying them with tunics and cloaks (compare Luke 3:11). The grieving community sent for Peter. He knelt down and prayed, then commanded her: "Tabitha, rise up" (v. 40; compare Mark 5:41). Peter used this verb to heal Aeneas (v. 34) and also to describe God's raising Jesus from the dead (Acts 2:24, 30, 32). The resuscitating power of God operates through the risen Jesus and now through Peter. It is the abiding healing power in the community of believers. Indeed resuscitation is a major activity of holy men in other traditions as well, e.g., Apollonius of Tyana resuscitates a young girl who died at the hour of marriage (Philostratus, *Life of Apollonius of Tyana* IV.45).

Restoration to life stories pose the biggest challenge to modern interpreters. All agree that with the exception of Lazarus who was "dead" four days (John 11), there is insufficient information in the reports to determine whether true death as understood in modern terms had actually occurred, or whether this was some comatose condition mimicking death. At least some medical specialists concede that at least some of the reports may well be referring to real death (the Lazarus story, for instance; Howard 2001: 188). It is sufficient for our purposes to acknowledge that Tabitha was indeed restored to life, to normal functioning. At the same time, the resonances of this story with the Elijah/Elisha cycle (1 Kgs 17:17-24 and 2 Kgs 4:32-37) clearly present Peter as a prophet just as the same resonances did for Jesus in the Gospels.

For reflection:

1. How important is it to know whether or not those raised from the dead were truly dead? Would that in any way lessen the significance or importance of what the healer did?

2. Twice in these stories and three times in total, members of the community are called "holy ones" (saints; Acts 9:13, 32, 41). How did they become holy ones? What can one expect from holy ones? What might holy ones expect from God and God's ministers (apostles, prophets)?

Acts 9:43–10:23 On a tanner's rooftop in Joppa

Just as a "double vision" shared earlier by Paul and Ananias served to provide both visionaries with new insight, so here another "double vision" provides Cornelius and Peter with new insight. Joppa may put a different twist on Peter as Apostle. It was from Joppa that Jonah sought to escape God's assignment for him to bring God's message to non-Israelites (Jonah 1:3). And here at Joppa, the Apostle Peter, who was reluctant to associate in table fellowship with non-Israelites, begins a journey toward a new appreciation of these same people. The irony here is that Peter is lodging with Simon, a tanner. In the Israelite tradition, this was an "unclean" occupation. Peter will learn some new lessons about the meaning of clean and unclean.

Acts 10:1-8 Cornelius' vision

Two sets of framing verses (10:1-2, 22) introduce us to Cornelius. He is a devout, upright, God-fearer who gave alms to Israelites liberally and prayed constantly to God. As a God-fearer, Cornelius was similar to the Ethiopian eunuch. Yet Cornelius was not circumcised or baptized, hence he would be considered marginal and even unclean. This helps understand the point of Peter's vision. A centurion of the Italian Cohort, Cornelius is a non-Israelite. Centurions typically earned sixteen times what a soldier earned, so Cornelius was in a position to be magnanimous or greedy and exploitive. What Peter accomplishes with Cornelius in this story somewhat preempts Paul's mission.

Cornelius was praying at 3:00 P.M. (the ninth hour), one of the times in the day set aside by Israelites for prayer. It was the same hour at which Peter and John customarily went up to the Temple for prayer (Acts 3:1). During his prayer, Cornelius had a waking vision in which he saw an angel of God who addressed him by name: "Cornelius." He "looked intently" at the angel. As previously noted (see Acts 1:10; 3:4; 7:55), that

Greek word "stare" or "look intently" is typically used by Luke in describing altered states of consciousness experiences. Further, Cornelius' reaction to the vision is typical: he was "seized with fear." The visionary does not usually recognize the one appearing, though in this report Cornelius, a God-fearer would be familiar with angels and seems to recognize the visitor from the realm of God. Nevertheless, most visionaries are understandably frightened.

In nearly all vision reports in the Bible (and elsewhere), the one appearing at first calms the visionary ("take heart; fear not!") and then discloses identity ("it is I"; see e.g., Luke 24:38-39). The angel tells Cornelius that his behavior (prayers and alms) have pleased and satisfied God (if not the Israelite leaders). The angel then instructs Cornelius to send emissaries to Joppa to bring Peter to Caesarea, even giving details of Peter's lodging. Notice that Cornelius immediately summons two servants and a devout soldier (quite likely another God-fearer), relates everything to them, and sends them on their way. We should note that they do not find Cornelius' experience strange or irrational. They obediently act upon the Centurion's command, fully understanding what altered states of consciousness experiences mean in their culture.

For reflection:

1. Notice how often in Acts the vision or altered state of consciousness experience occurs in conjunction with prayer (Acts 3:1; 4:31; 7:59; 8:15; 9:11; 10:2 to this point, and still more later in Acts). What lesson might a modern believer draw from this? Would this insight contribute to an improved appreciation for liturgical prayer?

Acts 10:9-16 Peter's vision

Still lodging at the house of Simon, the tanner, Peter goes up to the rooftop to pray at noon. At this point in the storyline of

Acts, noon is no longer an unusual time for a Mediterranean person to be out in the heat of the day. A modern Italian proverb reflects the Mediterranean understanding of noon. The only ones out in the heat of the day are: "cani ed Americani" (dogs and American tourists). Midday is time for *riposo, siesta*, a nap. The reader of Acts, however, has learned to expect that it will be a moment of illumination for those involved in the story. Peter was hungry. We have already learned that sensory deprivation such as fasting is practiced by many who desire to have a trance experience (recall Acts 9:9; Gore 1995: 10; Goodman 1990: 44). In the ancient, classical world silence, fasting, praying, lack of sleep over a long period of time, self-mutilation, sleeping on a skin of a sacrificed animal or in contact with some holy object, or sleeping in a holy place were techniques used to induce an altered state of consciousness. Peter is ripe for the experience, and indeed he falls into a trance.

The Greek word translated as trance (Acts 10:10) is *ekstasis* (ecstacy). But not every trance is ecstasy in the Greek sense of the word (see Rouget 1985: 11). It is the specific context of the experience that determines ecstasy. In the contemporary world, anthropologists propose that the most common context for ecstasy might be called "religious" (Gore 1995: 5). Since in the ancient world, religion was embedded in kinship (domestic religion, the home and family) and politics (political religion, the Temple), the proper context for ecstasy was not religion but rather dealing with the realm of God and the spirits. This difference of viewpoint causes modern readers to identify this activity with the occult, since it does not fit the prevailing paradigms of valid or "normal" perception. Peter was praying, that is, communicating with God, when he slipped into his trance or altered state of consciousness and saw a vision (Acts 11:5) in which God imparted new insight to him. Paul fell into a trance or ecstasy as he was praying in the Temple after returning to Jerusalem (Acts 22:17), and in this ecstatic vision, Jesus advised him to flee in order to preserve his life. (The other four occurrences of *ekstasis* in the New Testament [Mark 5:42; 16:8;

Luke 5:16; Acts 3:10] are not associated with a vision and are more appropriately translated "amazement," "astonishment," "awe." The Greeks were convinced that only one who is beloved by the gods and whose soul is god-loving experiences ecstasy. Perhaps this helps us to sharpen our appreciation of the voice from the sky that identified Jesus as a "beloved or chosen" son (Mark 9:7; Matt 17:5; Luke 9:35).

In his vision Peter saw something like a great sheet descending from the opened sky containing all kinds of animals, reptiles, and birds. A voice tells him: "Get up, Peter. Slaughter and eat." Peter declines: "Certainly not, sir. For never have I eaten anything profane and unclean." The voice replies: "What God has made clean, you are not to call unclean" (Acts 10:13-15, author's translation). This was repeated three times, and then the object went back into the sky.

Some scholars suggest that Peter's vision of the sheet may have been prompted by sails he saw from this house on the seacoast on the Mediterranean. This is a plausible and probable explanation. Often the images in a vision repeat what one has recently experienced in ordinary reality or in a dream. In the vision or trance, however, what the visionary sees is always reconfigured, reinterpreted. If Peter saw a sail on the sea, it is now a sheet containing food settling on the earth. The dialogue is chiastically arranged:

> Peter: anything (a) profane and (b) unclean
> God: (b') had made clean. . . (a') not to call profane (Acts 10:14-15)

This dramatic proclamation of the point, three times no less, leaves Peter "in doubt" or confused (v. 17).

One can only chuckle at Peter's perplexity. Three times in the story we are told that Peter's host in Joppa is a tanner (9:43; 10:6, 32). Tanning required the use of urine, and tanners reeked of this odor. This is why ancient laws required that tanyards be located at least 50 cubits outside of city walls. Simon the tanner's home was located near the seashore, not because he was wealthy or privileged, but rather to benefit from more pleasant sea breezes. Moreover, tanners were considered to be members of one of the "despised" professions. They were also considered unclean as were their workplaces. Peter, who stayed with this tanner for some time (Acts 9:43), must certainly have had the smell permeate his clothes. Yet he told God he has never "eaten" anything unclean. Peter apparently saw no contradiction between associating with this unclean fellow-member of the house of Israel, yet refusing to eat unclean foods. Worse, Peter was about to discover that while he associated with an unclean fellow-member of the house of Israel, he was still unwilling to associate with non-Israelites who believed in Jesus because non-Israelites were unclean people (see Gal 2:11-14). Only a trance experience of divine provenance could bring such a "believer" as Peter to his senses.

For reflection:

1. Luke's report of Peter's experience reveals him denying God's statement three times. "Eat." "I don't eat unclean food." "Don't call unclean what I made clean." It is not likely that this has any relationship to his three-fold denial of Jesus, but how could Peter be so bold as to deny God's explicit instruction repeatedly? What reason would Peter have to deny God's command?

2. In Leviticus 11, Moses presents God's rules about clean and unclean foods. In Peter's vision, God changes the rules. Since God is in charge, God can change the rules. How would this change affect those who lived before this point but failed to observe the rules? And what about those who did observe the rules that now were changed?

Acts 10:17-23 Interpretation of Peter's vision

Notice Peter's doubt or perplexity about what the vision might mean. All trance experiences require interpretation;

their meaning is not immediately self-evident. Cognitive neuroscience helps us understand why interpretation is needed. At a physiological level, in trance, the human organism most often relies for responses on templates learned and remembered in the brain and nervous system at the earliest instance of an experience. The memories, however, are not stored whole and entire but are spread out piece-meal over nodes in the brain. In trance, it seems that the memories are recombined into new patterns that require fresh interpretation. What is a reader to think about Peter's experience in Mark 7:1-23 (notably v. 19), and his puzzlement at his vision? Is it possible that Peter forgot how often Jesus ate with tax collectors and sinners (unclean people)? Perhaps he did, or perhaps his physiological pathways did not retrieve this information properly when he needed it. Whatever the explanation, Peter like all visionaries, required help in understanding and interpreting his vision. That help was at hand.

In what may be another trance, or Peter's return to a deeper level of trance, the Spirit told him about the arrival of the three emissaries whom the Spirit had sent earlier (Acts 10:19-20; recall v. 5). Peter was quite likely even more perplexed. His vision contained no such information. Hence he asked: "What is the reason for your being here?" (Acts 10:21). The men tell Peter about Cornelius (v. 22), indicating that an angel instructed him to summon Peter. If nothing else at this point, Peter realized that God is up to something. Messengers from God's realm communicated with Cornelius and with Peter. The messages are coordinated. The messengers have arranged a meeting between Peter and Cornelius, a non-Israelite. Meanwhile Peter invited these unclean people into his unclean lodging and hosted them! What was he thinking? Perhaps some time before they departed for Caesarea about thirty miles away, the point may have begun to sink in for Peter.

Acts 10:23-48 Soldier's house in Caesarea

Cornelius was expecting the arrival of his guest, Peter, and summoned kinsmen and close friends to meet and hear him. Peter reminded his host that it is against Torah for a member of the house of Israel to associate with or visit a non-Israelite. But "God has shown me that I should not call any person profane or unclean" (Acts 10:28). This insight was not really spelled out so clearly in Peter's vision (10:11-16). We can expect such gaps in high context documents such as the Bible in general and Acts in particular. Our growing knowledge and awareness of trance experiences, however, helps us to fill in what Peter and his associates knew, and what Luke, whether he knew well or not at all, didn't feel necessary to report in extensive detail. Peter's statement here makes it obvious that at some point between his vision and his arrival in Caesarea. Luke has Peter interpret his vision. It was not just about clean and unclean foods but about judging people to be clean or unclean. God's approach to human beings was already familiar in the tradition, the latent discourse upon which Peter could draw to interpret a vision. ". . . with the LORD, our God, there is no injustice, no partiality, no bribe-taking" (2 Chr 19:7; see also Job 34:19; Wis 6:7). Perhaps it was by recalling these statements from the tradition that Peter succeeded in understanding and interpreting his vision as God intended it.

Peter asked Cornelius why he summoned him. Now it was Cornelius' turn to share his vision with Peter. He identified the providential coincidence of time: Cornelius' vision took place at 3:00 P.M., and Peter arrived at Cornelius' home at the same hour (v. 30). One significant contrast between this report (vv. 30-32) and the original report (vv. 3-5) was that Cornelius now described the angel (v. 3) as "a man in bright apparel" (v. 30, RSV) echoing Luke's description of the messengers who addressed the women at the empty tomb (Luke 24:4). This may well be Lukan redactional activity, yet it is in perfect accord with the general interpretation. Cornelius' visitor in trance was a being from the realm of God, from alternate reality. In answer to Peter's question, Cornelius said this gathering has come together "to listen to all that you have been commanded by the Lord" (v. 33).

Peter's "speech" is decidedly theocentric. He mentions God six times. The speeches in Acts leave no doubt that God is in charge. Peter tells about what God has done through Jesus Christ and his Apostles on behalf of the Israelites but also "every nation." The entire episode repeats the word "all" and "every" with great impact (vv. 34-35, 43). Especially noteworthy in Peter's speech is this comment: "This man God raised [on] the third day and granted that he be visible, not to all the people but to us, the witnesses chosen by God in advance, who ate and drank with him after he rose from the dead" (Acts 10:40-41).

Peter's observation that God made Jesus visible only "to us" and "not to all the people" is not a statement of discrimination or unfairness on the part of God. God is the one who "hardwired" human beings with the capacity for varieties of consciousness, and God can also select the subjects of specific experiences. Sometimes God can even communicate with "enemies" in an altered state of consciousness (e.g., Nebuchadnezzar in Dan 2). At other times, as the mystical tradition reports, God withholds communication (the "dark night"). While all human beings are indeed capable of the experiences, the experiences will always be individual and culture specific.

Peter also observed that they ate and drank with the risen Jesus. This is not a literary device but rather the report of an actual experience. The reference points back to the episode reported by Luke (24:41-43) in which the risen Jesus ate a piece of broiled fish with his disciples. As already noted above (see p. 16), some contemporary biblical scholars ask whether Jesus really ate the fish. And they respond with a resounding "No, dead people have no need of nourishment!" Yet in the Israelite tradition, holy men (*ḥasidim* and *ṣedaqim*) could expect "quickening of the dead" (resurrection from the dead) and could expect to eat at three legged golden tables in the world to come

(Pilch 1998a). In the Israelite tradition, this phrase, "the world to come" points to that place where the righteous will go after they die and depart from "this world." Resurrection works a transformation of a person in their way of being, and in this tradition, it seems that even eating is transformed. Psychological anthropologists call that world "alternate reality," in contrast to this world which is ordinary reality, or culturally "normal" reality. Goodman calls alternate reality "the twin" of material reality (Gore 1995: x). It is noteworthy that Peter could share this information about eating with the risen Jesus to an audience that was predominantly non-Israelite without fear of skepticism or ridicule. Trance is a familiar experience in the circum-Mediterranean cultural world.

Finally, Peter reports the consequences of seeing the risen Jesus in an altered state of consciousness. The Apostles were commissioned to preach and testify to Jesus as appointed by God to judge the living and the dead. Anthropologists observed that two common results of alternate states of consciousness experiences are (1) the visionary finds a solution to a problem, or (2) is strengthened to embark on a new path in life. Clearly Peter and the Apostles experienced the second effect.

Peter's speeches in Acts of the Apostles tend to become long. Here after a brief while, the Spirit interrupted him by falling on those gathered, namely, the non-Israelites and gifting them with ecstatic utterance (glossolalia). It is quite evident that this is exactly what Luke has in mind here, and not speaking in foreign languages (xenoglossy) as he intimated in Acts 2. Once again it is well for us to notice that while human beings are not only capable of preparing themselves for trance, inducing and experiencing it, making contact with the Spirit world depends on the willingness of the inhabitants of God's realm to accept the invitation. In this episode, the Spirit took the initiative, as will occur more and more frequently as the narrative continues. The response of Peter's circumcised associates, that is, Israelite believers in Jesus is important. They knew these non-Israelites were not circumcised and hence lacked an important qualification for pleasing God, or so they thought, just as the Ethiopian eunuch had been marginalized by the house of Israel for his lack of physical qualification to please God (according to Israelite tradition). If the Spirit chose to fall on these non-Israelites and gift them, how could anyone refuse them full membership into the community of those who believed in Jesus? They were baptized forthwith.

For reflection:

1. Notice that Peter has two trance experiences (Acts 10:10, 19) separated by a return to ordinary waking consciousness (Acts 10:17). Anthropologists and neuroscientists point out that the continuity of consciousness is an illusion. How many times a day are you aware of shifting levels of awareness? Does this ever occur in prayer? At liturgy?

2. Notice also how interpretation of the vision is an ongoing process. Each time the visionary mulls over the vision, she or he remembers something new and adds it to the interpretation (compare Acts 11:16 with Acts 10:46-48). Compare this to personal experience where the meaning of an event unfolds over time. How does this ongoing reinterpretation of a personal experience compare to the differing interpretations siblings sometimes give to the memory of one and the same experience that they shared?

3. How do you explain that God shows no partiality yet allows only some to see the risen Jesus? Might the vision depend on God's willingness to disclose self or Jesus to some and not to others? Or is this Peter's explanation of why some see the risen Jesus and others don't?

Acts 11:1-18 Peter recapitulates his experience in Jerusalem

News of Peter's behavior in Caesarea traveled quickly via the gossip network to Jerusalem. When Peter arrived, circumcised believers challenged him for visiting and eating with un-circumcised people. Peter explained it to them "step by step" (Acts 11:4). He repeated his vision, and his initial interpreta-tion that missed the point. But either Luke or Peter has intro-duced some changes in the report that are nevertheless consonant with typical trance experience and its interpreta-tion. In Peter's report, the angel told Cornelius that Peter will "speak words to you by which you and all your household will be saved" (Acts 11:14; compare 10:5). Finally, in telling how the holy Spirit fell on these new believers, Peter remem-bered a word of the Lord (Acts 1:5). As already noted, the vi-sion is never a linear experience. The visionary must impose ✔ order upon what was seen. The visionary also supplies the soundtrack, usually by drawing upon tradition, the latent dis-course of the visionary's culture, ideology, or something simi-lar. Finally, the visionary mulls over the experience adding clearer interpretation as it occurs to her or him.

While the reminiscence of the word of the Lord could be a Lucan editorial touch, it could also reflect Peter's ongoing inter-pretation of his experience. Notice the conclusion: "When they heard this, they stopped objecting and glorified God. . . ." (Acts 11:18). Once again, it is significant that no one denied the vision. Instead, they found Peter's interpretation convincing and attained with Peter a new insight: "God has then granted life-giving repentance to the Gentiles too" (Acts 11:18).

Acts 11:19-30 Barnabas in Antioch and Jerusalem

Once again the mother community at Jerusalem sends someone (Barnabas) to investigate "the great number [in Anti-och] who believed and turned to the Lord" (Acts 11:21) just as it earlier had sent Peter and John (Acts 8:14) to investigate Philip's preaching success. Here at Antioch, the Hellenists who had fled Jerusalem proclaimed the Lord Jesus to other Greek-speaking members of the house of Israel (Hellenists, the reading preferable to Greeks in v. 20). They experienced great success. Barnabas, himself a Hellenist from Cyprus (Acts 4:36), rejoiced when his investigation proved that these new believers were indeed trustworthy. He exhorted them to continued loyalty to the Lord. To get qualified assistance in teaching these new believers, Barnabas went to Tarsus (more than a hundred miles away) to find a fellow Greek-speaking believer, Saul, with whom he returned to Antioch. They met with the believers and taught them over a period of a year.

An almost "throw away" line by Luke carries enormous significance. "It was in Antioch that the disciples were first called Christians" (Acts 11:26). The passive voice is important. That Greek name "Christian" was not a self-designation. It was imposed by outsiders. The insiders identified themselves as followers of "the Way" (Acts 9:2; 19:9, 23; 24:14). The Greek word Christian appears only three times in the New Testament and is always used by outsiders chiefly with a disapproving connotation (Acts 11:26; 25:8; 1 Pet 4:16). From a historical perspective, the term should not be used prior to the time of Constantine. The term "Christian," as it is understood today, emerged only from the christological debates of the fourth century after Constantine, especially the question: "How did Jesus of Nazareth relate to YHWH, the God of Israel?" (see Pilch 1999: 98–104). Hence in these reflections we refer to believers in Jesus as Messianists, that is, those who accepted Jesus as Messiah. We are grateful to Luke (Acts 11:26) for reminding us that outsiders applied the term "Christian" to these people.

During the teaching activity of Barnabas and Saul, prophets from Jerusalem visited Antioch, and one of them, Agabus, "predicted by the Spirit" a severe, worldwide famine in the rule of Claudius (A.D. 41-54). Like all prophetic messages, so, too, that of Agabus came to him from God in an altered state of consciousness experience. In this cultural world, no one knows the future except God and that one to whom God reveals it (compare the interesting parallel in the Joseph story: Gen 41:16, 39). Jesus himself testified: "Of that day or hour, no one knows, neither the angels in heaven, nor the Son, but only the Father" (Mark 13:32). The Antioch believers resolve to send assistance to the Jerusalem community through Barnabas and Saul.

ACTS 12:1-25 PETER, PRISONER IN JERUSALEM

The story of Peter's escape from prison (Acts 12:5-19) is sandwiched between two "Herod" snippets (12:1-4, the murder of James; 12:20-23, God's vengeance for that murder: the death of Herod). It was the days of unleavened bread (Acts 12:3), and the events take place in a prison (Acts 12:4-11), a private home (Acts 12:12-17), and a public arena (Acts 12:20-23), with gates (boundary points) between the areas (12:10, 14). In other words, we can map Peter's release through a sequence of inside/outside moves. Herod's prison (12:5-9, inside); prison gate leading to the city (12:10, outside); city street (12:10, outside); private gate leading into a private house (12:13-14, outside); Mary's house (12:16, inside).

Acts 12:1-4 Herod kills James

Historically this is Herod Agrippa I, Herod the Great's grandson, appointed king of all of Israel from A.D. 41–44 by Claudius Caesar. When his execution of James, the brother of John (sons of Zebedee), proved popular with members of the house of Israel, he arrested Peter before Passover. Memory of Peter's successful preaching at the feast of Passover might have prompted Herod to take this step. Peter had clearly announced that "God raised this Jesus. . . . [And] has made him both Lord and Messiah, this Jesus whom you crucified" (Acts 2:32, 36). Herod might well have been aware of the traditions recorded in an Aramaic version of the Torah reading for Passover. The Targum on Exodus 12:42 recalls four special nights mentioned in the Book of Memorials. "The four nights: when the world reaches its end to be redeemed: the yokes of iron shall be broken and the generations of wickedness shall be blotted out; and Moses will go up from the desert and the king Messiah from on high. One will lead at the head of the flock, and the other will lead at the head of the flock, and his Word will lead between the two of them, and I and they will proceed together. This is the night of Passover to the name of the Lord: it is a night reserved and set aside for the redemption of all the generations of Israel." Could this be the Passover at which the risen Jesus Messiah will return and redeem Israel? One way to dim people's memories of Peter's preaching would be to put him in prison and then execute him publicly after Passover.

Acts 12:5-19 Peter escapes in an altered states of consciousness experience

The reference to Passover in v. 4 gently hints to the reader resonances of that feast that might be expected in this account. The fact that the Church prayed fervently on his behalf heightened the expectation that God will somehow rescue Peter.

God doesn't fail to respond to the community prayer. Peter's imprisonment seems quite secure. Four squads were assigned to guard him, a fresh one for each watch of the night. He sleeps between two soldiers, is chained with two chains, and two soldiers stand guard at the door. The night before Herod intended to bring Peter to trial, "the angel of the Lord stood by him and a light shone in the cell" (Acts 12:7). The light indicates two things. One, it is associated with God and the realm of God hence understandably it accompanied this being from the realm of God. Two, light (white) is the color associated with the neurological change accompanying a change in awareness, a trance experience.

The angel "tapped" Peter on the side to waken him. The Greek word translated "tapped" is the same one that tells how Herod was killed: struck by a lethal "tap" (Acts 12:23, author's translation). It also described how God freed the Israelites from Egypt: the LORD smote their first-born in Egypt (Exod 12:29). Thus the same gesture by a being from the realm of God can be gentle or lethal, liberating or fatal.

Notice that Peter has difficulty determining whether this is "real" or a "vision" (v. 9). The translation is correct, but our modern understanding of altered states of consciousness helps us to interpret Peter's difficulty with greater cultural plausibility. The entire cosmos consists of two realities: ordinary, in which we live; alternate in which our deceased live together with God and spirits. Both dimensions are real, and events that happen in either dimension are real. As we noted earlier in this book, when Peter walks on the sea in a trance experience, in alternate reality, in order to meet Jesus walking on the sea, that is a real experience (Mark 6:45-51). It is really taking place in alternate reality. When his consciousness reverts to ordinary reality, he sinks. That part of the experience is also real. People who talk in their sleep say intelligible things that make sense in the dream. Anyone who hears this speech but doesn't know the dream will be confused. But to the dreamer, it all makes sense and upon awakening, the dreamer has to separate the dream from the waking moment. People who see departed loved ones in dreams insist that the presence and communication was as real as the waking moment when the loved one is no longer perceived. Experiences in alternate reality often have an impact and influence on ordinary reality. And telling the two realms apart sometimes becomes difficult for those accustomed to experiencing trance.

What exactly happened in this episode? The narrative reports that Peter's chains fell from his wrists, and he followed the angel out of prison. Since Peter very likely saw the light that shone in his cell, he knew he was in an altered state of consciousness. Did the light that shone in the cell blind the guards (v. 7)? Not necessarily. Recall that the blinding light that Paul saw did not blind his fellow travelers (Acts 22:9). If the guards were not in trance, they saw neither the light nor the escape. We are familiar with biblical stories in which some have an ASC while others in their company do not (John 12:27-30). In trance, in alternate reality, Peter and the angel " passed the first guard, then the second." The gate leading to the city opened of its own accord (v. 10).

Since Peter ultimately got free, something like this had to happen. It is easier, at least for those cultures open to the experience, to explain this event in terms of ecstatic trance than to deny it in terms of the so-called "laws of nature" (see Goldman 1999). If the gates were not secured, the "laws of nature" worked perfectly in this story! But this is hardly plausible given all the other "laws of nature" elements in this story which would require explanation (chains being loosened, all the guards failing to perceive anything, etc.). Eventually Peter and the angel emerged, found an alley, and the angel disappeared (Acts 12:10). Peter was free.

In all trance experience, the participation of the spirit world is welcome and hoped for. In trances reported in the Bible, someone from the realm of God interacts with human beings in ordinary reality. If spirits from the realm of God (Angel of the Lord; God) were not involved in Peter's trance, he may well have remained in chains and wakened from a frustrating dream. Instead, when Peter "recovered his senses" (Acts 12:11), that is, when he was no longer in an altered state of consciousness but in ordinary, waking consciousness, and realized he was outside the prison, free, he said, "Now I know for certain that [the] Lord who sent his angel and rescued me. . . ." (Acts 12:11). That Peter was truly free convinced him it could only be the work of God.

It is worth repeating the reflection of anthropologist Dr. Robinette Kennedy (*As the Crow Flies* vol. 2, #1. Winter 2001) mentioned relative to Peter's first escape from prison (Acts 5:19). She reported that some subjects who in trance take spirit journeys fasten their body in ordinary reality so that it would be waiting for them upon their return. "Supposedly, Houdini could perform genuine feats of magic because of his training in levitation techniques from the same Western Asian shamanic traditions (Siberia and Mongolia), which allowed his spirit to survive while his body withstood remarkable physical trials. When he would return to his body, which he had left in a life-threatening situation, he would find *the ropes untied and the locks opened.*"

When Peter arrived at Mary's house (Acts 12:12-17), the events took a comical turn. The maid who heard Peter's voice at the door didn't open it. She left him standing and knocking while she went instead to tell the gathering. The people refused to believe her saying she was "out of her mind" or seeing "his angel." Again, we notice the range of explanations for their experiences available to our ancestors in faith. "Out of your mind" is a judgment that places blame on the reporter; she is mistaken or confused. But if she speaks truthfully, then she is likely perceiving a being from alternate reality, the realm of God: "his angel." Two different assessments. Yet "his angel" is believable to them because the realm of God and its inhabitants were part of one reality, the same one in which mortals live. As modern research confirms, alternate reality and its inhabitants are not far from ordinary reality. Dr. Goodman points out that these are parallel realities (Gore 1995: x).

When he finally joined the community that was praying for him, Peter explained how the Lord had led him out of prison. Once again we notice how with the passage of even a brief period of time, his interpretation changed. At first he said the Lord sent his angel (v. 11), and now he attributes his rescue directly to God (v. 17). His understanding and interpretation of his experience sharpened and improved. He charged the group to report his experience to James, the brother of the Lord (who heads the Jerusalem community), and left for another place. Meanwhile when Herod learns of the escape and cannot find Peter, he ordered the guards to be executed. The fact that Herod put to death the guards who could not explain how Peter escaped (Acts 12:18-19) indicates that Peter really did escape. While it is possible that Luke has embellished a tradition to demonstrate God's providence, many of the elements of his narrative are consonant with similarly documented trance experiences.

Acts 12:20-25 Herod dies

Herod left Jerusalem for Caesarea where a group from Tyre and Sidon came to seek food from him. Perhaps the famine predicted by Agabus was already beginning. Josephus said that Herod loved to wear silver royal robes that glistened in the sun. When he addressed the crowd, they shouted: "This is the voice of a god, not of a man" (v. 22). Mediterranean cultural values dictate that such public compliments must be denied by the one to whom they are directed. Surely all the more when the compliment makes a deity out of a mortal. Herod made no such denial, but God will not be mocked. God's angel struck him dead because he did not behave in prescribed cultural fashion and attribute the honor to God but kept it for himself. In two transitional verses Luke first notes how the word of God continued to spread, and then he brings Barnabas and Saul back into the story along with John Mark whom he just introduced.

For reflection:

1. Commentators sometimes describe Peter's rescue from prison as miraculous. What does that mean? What is a miracle? How would that escape be explained? If the escape happened in an altered state of consciousness, would that lessen the reputation or status of those from the realm of God who effected it? How do altered states of consciousness or trance experiences make God's intervention "more" plausible or "real"?

2. Are you familiar with the realm of God and its inhabitants? Which inhabitants are familiar to you? How do you communicate with them?

Chapter Four

Acts 13:1–21:36
Journeys into Non-Israelite Territory

Though it is customary to speak of three missionary journeys of Paul, scholars recognize that it is difficult to calculate these on the basis of Acts. Spencer (1997: 131) identifies an inclusion that helps discover a different outline for this segment of Acts. The report of "what God had done" or "accomplished" on behalf of the non-Israelites marks the beginning and end of this segment (Acts 14:27; 21:19). In general, this section can be divided into two segments: a Mediterranean Expedition (Acts 13:1–16:5) and Aegean Expedition (Acts 16:6–21:36). This division will facilitate our reflections.

ACTS 13:1–16:5 THE MEDITERRANEAN EXPEDITION

This section features proclamation as the dominant activity. In a sense Barnabas and Paul have been preparing for this activity in Antioch (Acts 11:25-26) for a whole year, meeting with and teaching a large company of people. Agabus, a Jerusalem prophet (Acts 11:27-28), by means of information obtained from the Spirit in an altered state of consciousness experience, the normal channel used by beings in the realm of God for communicating with human beings (1 Sam 3:1), foretold "a severe famine all over the world." The disciples determined to send help to those living in Judea through Barnabas and Paul (Acts 11:29). The conclusion of Acts 12 is better translated: "After Barnabas and Saul completed their relief mission in [or to] Jerusalem, they returned" (Acts 12:25). This translation is tenable on the basis of textual evidence and connects better with the next section.

Acts 13:1-3 Commission in Antioch

The Church at Antioch learned the will of the Spirit in a communal experience of trance (Acts 13:2). They (the entire community) are worshiping (the Greek word is the source of our English word "liturgy") and fasting. We already know that sensory deprivation such as fasting can contribute to the inducement of trance. Recall Saul's three-day fast in Acts 9:9; and Cornelius' four-day fast in Acts 10:20 (*textus receptus,* but not in modern Greek editions). Some scholars associate the fasting by the Antioch community (and others) with penance. This is plausible, but given the certain connection of fasting with altering levels of consciousness, it is perhaps more plausible that our ancestors in faith fasted in order to retain ready access to help from the realm of God.

The purpose of this trance is to select two men from the group of five prophets and teachers in the church at Antioch, namely, Barnabas and Saul for a service determined by the Spirit. Jerome Neyrey describes a "vocation commissioning" literary form that is commonly used in the Bible to authenticate different kinds of leaders. The form has two basic parts: an introduction, and the actual commissioning. In this instance, the introduction is the fact that the holy Spirit communicates to the community while they are fasting during worship. What is noteworthy in this report is that the community has no doubt of the identity of the one communicating (the holy Spirit), nor are they fearful or frightened (common responses in some instances of communication with the realm of God). Given the frequency of these trance experiences in Acts, it seems reasonable to conclude that the community and many if not all its members lived in a state of readiness, attuned to the realm of God, to alternate reality, open to prayer and heightened awareness of God. This includes familiarity with residents of the realm of God who elect to communicate with the community in ordinary reality.

The commission itself is straightforward: Barnabas and Saul are authenticated and legitimized for the Spirit's work. The commission is (1) formal: set apart for Barnabas and Saul, (2) sealed by the Spirit personally, (3) and involves preaching repentance and forgiveness of sins. The work is manifested and confirmed in the very next report (Acts 13:4-12).

For reflection:

1. Even before the Second Vatican Council, the length of the fast required before receiving the Holy Eucharist was changed. Previously, would-be recipients of the Eucharist (including the celebrant) were expected to fast from midnight to the time of reception on the next day. The fast was then changed to one hour before reception. While this change was certainly a welcome relief from hunger pangs human beings routinely experience upon awaking in the morning, it may also have reduced if not eliminated the effectiveness of a key element in inducing trance. Modern trancers eat lightly if at all before a trance session. Do you think it is a practice worth restoring in your personal life?

2. When Jesus was with the disciples, they did not fast. Jesus said that after he left them, they would fast (Luke 5:33-35). While he was with them in ordinary reality, Jesus and the disciples could communicate with each other readily. When Jesus ascended to the realm of God, the disciples could facilitate communication with him by fasting. How does this interpretation of Luke 5:33-35 match others familiar to you?

Acts 13:4-12 Contending in Cyprus

The first stop on the work schedule laid out by the holy Spirit is Cyprus. The preachers proclaim the word of God in the synagogues traversing the island in a southwesterly direction, arriving at Paphos. Here they meet with Bar-Jesus, a magician, also identified as a Judean false-prophet. This would mark him as someone who pretended to speak God's will for the here and now but was not an authentic spokesperson. Later (Acts 13:8) Luke mistakenly says that the name Bar-Jesus means Elymas. As we have learned, double names are common in this world, especially for Judeans. One name was for the Hebrew or Aramaic-speaking in-group (thus, Saul; Bar-Jesus), the other was for the Greek speaking out-group (Paul; Elymas). As previously noted, the popular myth that Paul underwent a name change from Saul to Paul after his conversion has no basis in the Scripture. The verse on which this opinion is inadequately based (Acts 13:9) is correctly translated here: "Saul, who is also called Paul."

We see the three (Barnabas, Saul-Paul, and John) preaching the word throughout Cyprus and then by invitation before Sergius Paulus, the pro-consul or provincial governor, and Bar-Jesus/Elymas, the magician. Instead of receiving the word with repentance and openness, Bar-Jesus resisted it and sought to dissuade the pro-consul also. At this point, Paul slips into trance ("looked intently at [Bar-Jesus]"—recall the comments at Acts 3:4) and gains additional insight into his opponent which in turn helps him to make a strong counter argument. Thanks to this new information, Paul labels Bar-Jesus negatively: "son of the devil, you enemy of all that is right, full of every sort of deceit and fraud" (13:10). Then Paul identifies the wrongdoing of which he should repent: "twisting the straight paths of [the] Lord" (13:10; contrast with Luke 3:4-5). This justifies Luke's labeling of him as a false prophet. According to Paul, this man's true identity is "son of the devil" and not "son of Jesus" as his name would indicate.

Spencer (1997: 139) rightly identifies this encounter as a contest about honor. The trio has invaded the magician's turf. He may have been a court magician now feeling threatened by the preaching that is persuasive to the pro-consul. More than that, Paul learned in trance and then declared that God will temporarily blind his opponent. Scholars note that Paul's behavior is the kind one might expect from Bar-Jesus, a magician. In the ancient world it was difficult to distinguish magic from mighty deeds of God (see Exod 7:9-12, 22; 8:7, 19). But by beating a "false prophet" (Acts 13:6) at his own game, Paul showed himself to be superior, therefore worthy of honor. Paul was thus authentically working in the name of God—he was a prophet just like Moses (Acts 13:11; compare Exod 100:21-29; Deut 28:28-29) and a messenger just like John who spoke the true word of God (Luke 3:3-5; Isa 40:3-5). When the pro-consul saw what took place, he was astonished at the teaching of the Lord!

How are we to understand the temporary blindness? As suggested in the story of Ananias and Sapphira (Acts 5:1-11), people in cultures that believe in the power of certain persons to heal or to hurt can be really effected as the authority intends (Howard 2001: 208–10). Here the authoritative command of Paul, a holy man acting in God's name, can plausibly cause temporary blindness. This blindness is a type of conversion disorder sometimes called "hysterical blindness." Paul has the power to impose it and remove it.

For reflection:

1. One category of trance identified by Dr. Goodman is "divination," that is, an attempt to seek the answer to a question or a solution to a problem from alternate reality, the realm of God. In this instance, Paul seems to have done precisely this: he received a fuller appreciation of his opponent's true identity (answer to a question) and learned how God intended to deal with the problem posed by this opponent (inflict temporary blindness). Bar-Jesus' experience of blindness seems to reflect Paul's (Acts 9). Do you think Bar-Jesus later changed his life and found the straight way (see Acts 9:11)?

Acts 13:13-52 Proclaiming in Pisidia

Paul acted alone in the face off with Bar-Elymas in the presence of Sergius Paulus. Now Paul is mentioned as the leader

("Paul and his companions" Acts 13:13). They traveled to Pisidian Antioch where on the Sabbath they went to the assembly (NAB: Synagogue). There they were invited to present a "word of exhortation" (Acts 13:15, RSV) after the reading of the law and prophets. Until the year 200, the synagogue was not a place of worship so much as a community center where men would gather to read and discuss Scripture, among other topics (Pilch 1999: 99–100). This was not a worship service since none yet existed for this place. The Temple still stands.

Paul's speech reflects elements of previous speeches in Acts (all Lucan creations), with some additions. He skips over the Patriarchal period but mentions King Saul (first time in Acts), perhaps because of an association with his own Hebrew name. Yet as in previous speeches, so, too, here Paul's main focus is God and what God has done for and in Jesus. God brought Jesus to Israel as savior (v. 23). Inhabitants and leaders of Jerusalem failed to recognize Jesus as the fulfillment of the prophets "read Sabbath after Sabbath" (v. 27). They had him put to death, but God raised him from the dead (vv. 30, 33, 37), and he appeared to his Galilean disciples in altered states of consciousness experiences. The triple repetition of God's raising Jesus is a powerful statement that Jesus and his activities were pleasing to God. In Jesus, "every believer is justified" (Acts 13:39), something the Law was unable to do. In conclusion, Paul cites Habakkuk (1:5) as a warning against rejecting the message.

As usual, many in the group believed and accepted. In fact, they invited them to return on the following Sabbath. But others were "filled with jealousy" (v. 45). The reason for this is that if Paul and his companions gain honor, fame, reputation, that of the Judaic leaders diminishes. They literally "blasphemed" Paul and contradicted what he said. This was a challenge. Paul does not engage in riposte, but rather declared what he learned from God in trance: "The Lord has commanded us, 'I have made you a light to the (non-Israelites) Gentiles, that you may be an instrument of salvation to the ends of the earth'" (v. 47). This statement was not reported in either of the three accounts of Paul's call and commission (Acts 9; 22; 26). Actually, it sounds more like what the risen Jesus said to Ananias who restored sight to Paul (Acts 9:15-16). No doubt Ananias shared this with Paul. Or it is quite likely another Lucan creation or variation on the content of Paul's visions Nevertheless, Paul makes it clear that the source of his confidence is the assurances in communication he has had with God and the risen Jesus in trance. From the perspective of trance experience, Paul's statement fits well with a visionary's ever evolving and improving understanding of the content of his or her vision.

The non-Israelites are obviously delighted, while the prominent members of the house of Israel and leading men of the city expel Paul and Barnabas from the city. They "shook the dust from their feet in protest" (v. 51; compare Luke 9:5; 10:11) and journeyed toward Iconium "filled with joy and the holy Spirit" (v. 52). For them, the Spirit is the major communicator of God's will.

Acts 14:1-20 Miracle work in Lycaonia: a healing trance

The disciples proceeded southeast from Antioch to the region of Lycaonia, specifically to three neighboring cities: Iconium, Lystra, and Derbe. In Iconium they preached boldly and their words were confirmed by mighty deeds. The Lord granted "signs and wonders to occur through their hands" (Acts 14:3). Typically, response was divided. Some were favorable, others determined to attack and stone them causing the two to flee.

In Lystra, Paul healed a man who was a cripple from birth (Acts 14:8-10). The healing is very similar to that of Peter in Acts 3. Both sick men are described by the same phrase: "a man crippled from birth," "a crippled man, lame from birth" (Acts 3:2; 14:8). Peter and Paul "looked intently (stare, gaze)" at the men before raising them (Acts 3:4; 14:9). In other words, both healers entered a trance, no doubt a healing trance, one of the categories identified by Dr. Goodman (Gore 1995:41-49). Both healed men confirmed their improved condition by leaping, walking, jumping / jumping up and walking (Acts 3:8; 14:10). Both healings are effected through "faith" (Acts 3:16; 14:9). Finally, both healing events took place near Temple gates (Acts 3:2, the Jerusalem Temple; Acts 14:13, the sacred place of Zeus).

Scholars identify a basic "literary" form in reporting such healing stories. The form includes an exposition (v. 8), the healer's word and gesture (v. 9-10), demonstration or proof of the healing (v. 10), and effect on the bystanders (vv 11-13). The form is evident in Peter's healing (Acts 3:1-11) and in similar stories. Some think that the story about Paul may be a repetition or transferal of Peter's story to enhance Paul's status. This interpretation is certainly possible and common on a literary level. Yet as we already noted about literary forms relative to the report of Paul's call and commission by God (Acts 9; 22; 26, see pp. 75–76 above), the texts we read report a predictable Mediterranean *cultural behavioral pattern*. Culture dictates how one should behave in a given situation; in this case, how a holy man (Peter, Paul) ought to behave in a healing situation. Their behaviors are not idiosyncratic. They are part of a rite.

The importance of ritual rite cannot be underestimated. If it is not performed precisely, the desired results, in this case healing, might not happen (Gore 1995: xi). Dr. Goodman considers ritual the bridge over which beings from the realm of God enter into our ordinary world (Goodman 1990: 55). Literary form particularly in healing stories seems most certainly to reflect a defined healing ritual rite.

Strelan (2000) has noted some key elements in this report which strongly correlate with trance experiences, particularly the stare and the loud voice. Recall what we mentioned above concerning the stare as an indication that a person may be in trance (pp. 40–41). Here Paul, a holy man (Acts 13:9, see 52 "filled with the holy Spirit" and 14:15 empowered to heal by the "living God"), fell into trance ("looked intently" at the lame man). In this state of consciousness, he gained an intuition into the crippled man's condition: "he had the faith to be healed" (literally "saved" or "rescued" Acts 14:9), and Paul restored him to wholeness. Strelan (2000: 492) also correctly suggests that Paul's physical condition, e.g., his breathing (strong breathing, or sighing) may have been altered. The magical papyri often recommend deep breathing, sighing, groaning, hissing, and other respiratory noises for the one who would work magic (e.g., PGM 7.768 and 13.946).

Yet another significant element that Strelan points out in this story is the identification of Paul as Hermes, a messenger with wings on his feet. According to Hippocrates, "opposites cure opposites" (Galen 8.698). A healer must have the proper spirit to heal the spirit of the cripple and the spirit causing the cripple's condition. Moreover, the ancients following Aristotle believed it was the soul that felt pain and not the body (Pilch 2003b: 22). Specifically, the sentient soul felt pain. Since this soul was considered to be coterminous with the body, a person mistakenly might think the body feels pain. Paul gazed into the soul of this man, saw his faith (=loyalty to the healer) to be healed (Acts 14:9), and made him well again.

Finally, the loud voice characterizes trances of holy men across cultures, specifically a change of voice or increase in tone and volume. Indeed, one ecstatic trance posture identified by Goodman, The Singing Shaman, begins with sound that changes during the trance (Gore 1995: 272–77). Dr. Goodman's research on glossolalia shows that shouting is typical in glossolalia experiences (Goodman 1972: vii, xvi, 15, 61, 81, 109). It is therefore plausible to suspect that a trance is occurring in instances where a loud voice is mentioned. For instance, Luke mentions a loud voice when describing those offering praise to God (e.g., Acts 17:15; 19:37). At hearing the voice of Mary, Elizabeth was "filled with the holy Spirit" and exclaimed her sentiments "with a loud cry" (Luke 1:41-42, RSV). This is an ecstatic cry, and Luke appropriately links Spirit-possession with the loud cry.

What exactly did Paul heal? While some believe the event happened exactly as reported, Howard (2002: 211–12) believes that as in the case of Peter's healing of a congenitally lame man this, too, is an abreactive treatment of a conversion disorder. Abreaction is the expression and emotional release of unconscious material such as a repressed idea or emotion especially in the presence of a healer. If the man's problem was actually psychosomatic, as some claim, releasing that which caused it would resolve the problem. The claim that the problem was congenital may be nothing more than Luke's habit of enhancing the healing.

For reflection:

1. Throughout Acts of the Apostles and the Bible, being filled with the Spirit is an important element for inducing trance. How does a believer invite the Spirit, become familiar with the Spirit, communicate with the Spirit to obtain the gifts of the Spirit? How does a believer open self to be filled with the Spirit if God so wills?

Acts 14:21-28 Nurturing the churches

The response to Paul's beneficence was mixed. His beneficiaries wanted to offer sacrifices (Acts 14:18), but fellow members of the house of Israel stoned him and left him for dead outside the city (Acts 14:19). Paul and Barnabas survived and continued their journey to Derbe, then retraced their steps to Lystra, and Iconium, returning finally to Antioch. Notice also that when appointing elders (presbyters) in every church, Paul and Barnabas routinely committed them to the Lord with prayer and fasting (Acts 14:23). There should be no doubt this was done with a view to entering trance and communicating with "the Lord in whom they had put their faith" (14:23). Unlike Antioch where the leaders were identified as teachers and prophets (Acts 13:1), these leaders were given the title "elders" which in Luke-Acts is used exclusively for authorities in the house of Israel. Perhaps this title of leaders in mixed congregations is intended to maintain a connection with the group in Jerusalem.

Acts 15:1–16:5 Evaluation in Jerusalem

While this account of dissension and conflict resolution in Jerusalem reads like a straightforward report, scholars agree that Luke has simplified a complex issue. We adopt Luke's approach to move our narrative forward. Pharisees who joined the Jesus group and accepted Jesus as Messiah came to Antioch and insisted that non-Israelites who join the community of believers should be circumcised according to Mosaic practice. (The practice actually traces back to Abraham! [Gen 17:11]). This challenged the work of Paul and Barnabas who are then dispatched to the Apostles and elders in Jerusalem to resolve the conflict.

Following a long debate, Peter spoke and reminded all present about God's will in the matter. Since God made no distinction between Israelites and non-Israelites but accepted both, why impose Judaic practices on non-Israelites? God has revoked God's own distinction between clean and unclean. The testimony of Paul and Barnabas concerning the mighty deeds worked by God among non-Israelites that followed Peter's speech confirmed what Peter has said.

James had the final word and resolved the debate and conflict. He, too, repeats that this is God's will, that is, to include non-Israelites in the divine plan. The compromise solution to facilitate tablefellowship and maintain a harmonious community of believers is that non-Israelites should observe those provisions of the Holiness Code which used to bind Israel's resident aliens (see Lev 17-18): refrain from meat offered to idols, refrain from food not slaughtered according to ritual (blood, strangled), and intercourse with close kin. The decision was recorded in a letter to be delivered by Barnabas and

Paul, and Judas and Silas (=Silvanus, a companion of Paul on later travels).

Scholars agree that because this account is difficult, if not impossible, to square with Paul's own report in Galatians 2, Luke has taken considerable liberty in composing an irenic view of things as is his custom in Acts. The fact that the contents of this letter appear to be given later by James to Paul as something new (Acts 21:25) indicates that Luke has intentionally modified his sources in this regard.

Before we leave this so-called "Council" as it is often described, it is worth noting the central and authoritative position of James, especially with regard to Peter. Previously when Peter escaped from prison in an altered state of consciousness experience, he hinted at James' ascendancy to importance in the Jerusalem church by directing that a report be delivered to him (Acts 12:17). This James, of course, is not the brother of John, son of Zebedee. That James was murdered by Herod (Acts 12:2). This James is the brother of the Lord (see Gal 1:19; Matt 13:55). In Middle Eastern culture of antiquity and the present, family ties are paramount. Though one person may be king, the entire family rules and has a role in the administration. The West calls this nepotism and looks askance at it. In the Middle East, it is the proper thing to do. Take care of the family above all. Thus, since God raised Jesus from the dead and worked the divine will through Jesus, it makes good Middle Eastern sense that the family of Jesus should hold authoritative positions. In the case of Jesus, scholars call this phenomenon "Jewish Christianity," namely, that segment of the Jesus movement that retained many Israelite practices but realized that by designating Jesus as Messiah, God was doing something new. Franciscan archaeologist Bellarmino Bagatti, who excavated Nazareth extensively, pointed out that the family of Jesus continued to exist and rule the Church for some three centuries.

The commendatory letter on behalf of Paul, Barnabas, Silas, and Judas Barsabbas sent by the Jerusalem group after its meeting (Acts 15:23-29) makes an interesting comment about the group's conclusion: "It is the decision of the holy Spirit and of us . . ." that the non-Israelite recipients observe certain stipulations of the Holiness Code (Acts 15:28). They are in such frequent and intimate contact with the Spirit that the authors of the letter can speak like this, which might seem surprising to modern ears. Whether the group received their insight in an altered state of consciousness experience or not, they are vividly aware of the presence of the Spirit particularly when they determine something for the community that they are convinced God is shaping.

At this point in the story Paul and Barnabas part company (a bit more amicably than indicated in Gal 2:6). Barnabas took Mark with him and headed toward Cyprus. Paul chose Silas and traveled through Syria and Cilicia. In Lystra, Paul met Timothy, a disciple whose mother (see 1 Tim 1:5) was of the house of Israel (thus, in the opinion of some scholars, automatically making Timothy a member, too) but whose father was likely a Hellenized Israelite (i.e., Greek Israelite). Paul had him circumcised so that he would not encounter difficulties from other members of the house of Israel when he joined Paul and Silas as an associate. Luke presents Paul as an observant member of the house of Israel who still observes its practices but refuses to impose them on non-Israelites.

ACTS 16:6–21:36 THE AEGEAN EXPEDITION

This segment of the story presents five "public accusation type-scenes" with this sequence of events: (1) hostile seizure of the preachers and bringing them before a public tribunal, (2) explicit declaration of charges, and (3) violent reaction of protest and punishment from crowds and authorities. The direct accusations at the heart of each scene are quite pointed: Philippi, Greco-Roman fortune peddlers (Acts 16:20-21); Thessalonica, members of the house of Israel (Acts 17:6-7); Corinth, members of the house of Israel (Acts 18:13); Ephesus, Greco-Roman shrine traders (Acts 19:25-27); and Jerusalem, Asian members of the house of Israel (Acts 21:28). Deviant labeling is rife in all these episodes.

Acts 16:6-10 The commission in Troas

Paul, Silas, and Timothy promulgated the letter from the Apostles and elders in Jerusalem to the communities they visited on their travels through Asia Minor. The holy Spirit thwarted their travel plans twice in this itinerary! First, they intended to proceed from Syria and Cilicia into the province of Asia to the south and west, but the Spirit "prevented" them from preaching the word there. Next they wanted to go to the region of Bithynia to the north, but again the "Spirit of Jesus" did not allow them. There is no explicit indication that these insights came to Paul and his companions in trance. It is plausible, however, to think that they did. The message or inspiration from the Spirit might have come in a dream, a daydream, a meditation, or something similar. Recall that people can and do slip in and out of many different states of consciousness throughout a normal day.

An explicit trance experience is described in verse 9. It is a night vision, perhaps a dream. Paul sees a human being (not an angel or other spirit), a Macedonian, in a standing position inviting Paul to "come over to Macedonia and help us." In alternate reality one can see people one has never met before. Alternate reality does not contain the time and space dimensions of ordinary reality (Goodman 1990: 179–80). The people one meets in alternate reality, the realm of God, are chiefly those who reside there, including those who have died. But it is also possible in alternate reality to see people who still live in ordinary reality, even in a region far removed from the one having a trance. In this episode, Paul did not see a specific person with a name, but rather a person from a geographical region, a Macedonian. This is typical for people like Paul who is a collectivistic personality living in a collectivistic culture.

Such cultures tend to stereotype. To know one is to know all *(ab uno disce mnes)*. It is likely that he recognizes the man by his distinctive garb. The report also does not say that the man was standing in Macedonia. He was simply present to Paul in the night vision. Or, to use the language of trance interpretation, this is the meaning and interpretation that (Luke's) Paul imposed on the man he saw in trance.

Notice the instant interpretation and response. Paul concluded that "God had called us to proclaim the good news to them" (Acts 16:10). Immediately they sought passage from Troas to Macedonia. The ability to interpret trance varies with individuals. For Peter in the Cornelius episode, it took a while for Peter to understand and interpret that experience. The same was true for Paul in his experience on the road to Damascus. But at this point in the narrative, the experience has occurred often enough for the subjects to understand more quickly and respond immediately. With increased experience of alternate reality, the realm of God, visionaries become more familiar with it and find that it becomes easier to interpret their trances.

For reflection:

1. Have you ever experienced God's negative judgment about your plans, wishes, desires? How did you recognize that it was from God? When did you realize that God had a different plan?

2. What kind of frustration do you think this God-directed team felt to have their travel plans thwarted?

Acts 16:11-40 In Philippi

Paul and his associates arrived at Philippi and waited until the Sabbath so they could meet with fellow members of the house of Israel. On that day, they went outside the city "along the river where we thought there would be a place of prayer"

(Acts 16:13). It seems the Judaic population was too small to have a synagogue, but they did gather near a river for purposes of ritual ablution and prayer. This helps to understand why Paul found women gathered here for prayer (see Lev 15:19-33). The presence of Lydia, a dealer in purple cloth confirms this suggestion. Like tanning, so, too, purple dyeing involved the use of animal urine and was hence a very smelly process. Likely Lydia and her coworkers lived outside the city gates, too, where the business would also be located.

How could Paul and his male associates join the women in the rigidly gender divided world? Outdoors in general are male space, but in this instance, because the river was used for ablutions, the space could be viewed as female. However, once the function was finished, the space could be considered to revert to being male space or generic space available to men and women. The primary understanding and interpretation of the space would depend on the function it serves. Since Paul was teaching, the males have taken charge of this space. Women could be present since it is where the teacher was located.

The Lord rendered Paul's teaching effective for Lydia who was baptized along with her household. Some scholars have proposed that she gave an example to her household that they dutifully followed. This interpretation fails to understand collectivistic cultures and persons. Such cultures are group centered rather than individualistic. They promote conformity and consider uniqueness disruptive. The primary allegiance of people in such cultures is to others, and the primary obligation is to the development of the group. Self-promotion and development of one's potential is frowned upon. Behavior is dictated by the group's mores and sanctions or the leader's authority. That was certainly the case here with Lydia. It was her authoritative position that dictated that her household would be baptized along with her. She invited Paul and his associates to remain for a while and they did.

For reflection:

1. Individualism characterizes just 20% of the cultures on the face of our planet. Individualistic cultures hold isolating values. It would be rare indeed for a Western group (e.g., a family, or community) to behave like Lydia and her household. What are the advantages and disadvantages of individualism?

2. About 80% of cultures on our planet are collectivistic as described above. They hold congregating values. Can you identify advantages and disadvantages of collectivistic cultures?

3. Cultural specialists point out that the values of these two kinds of cultures (individualistic and collectivistic) are so totally integrated within each culture that it is impossible to transfer values from one culture and combine them with the values of the other. In other words, individuals in an individualistic culture will be unable to follow the example of individuals in collectivistic cultures. With regard to collectivistic cultures, therefore, what can individualists hope for? Understanding? More than understanding? Empathic understanding?

On the way to the prayer place one day, the group met a girl possessed, literally, by a "Pythian spirit" or "an oracular spirit." This spirit was believed to be a serpent or dragon that lived at the foot of Mount Parnassus and guarded the oracle of Delphi. Apollo slew this spirit. The anonymous girl thus spoke in a possession trance: "These people are slaves of the Most High God, who proclaim to you a way of salvation" (Acts 16:17). Those familiar with the biblical tradition know that even those possessed by hostile spirits often speak truth. Unclean spirits regularly recognized and stated the truth about Jesus (e.g., "the Son/Holy One of God") just before Jesus cast them out (Luke 4:33-34, 41; 8:28). Sometimes they asked to be left alone (Luke 4:34; 8:28). Since this girl spoke truth, why did Paul silence her? Quite likely not because of what she said but because of the source of its inspiration: a Pythian spirit. Paul freed her from that bondage. Howard (2001: 212–14) thinks the girl may have been mentally handicapped in some way or more likely that she was a trickster or a fraud whom Paul simply unmasked. To suit his purposes, according to Howard, Luke turned the event into an exorcism, though it lacks all features of such stories elsewhere in the New Testament.

For reflection:

1. In the Christian tradition there is longstanding advice to test the spirits (1 John 4:1). This episode illustrates the importance of so doing. How does one test the spirits?

2. What do you think of Paul's treatment of this girl? She disappears from the storyline. Did she become a believer? Does she find and enter the way of salvation? Does the local community of believers take her in?

3. It is popular in modern culture to speak metaphorically about problems in one's life as "demons" to be ejected. If this idea is congenial to you, from which "demons" do you feel the need to be freed?

The owners of the exorcized slave girl were understandably not pleased. In her new condition, "their hope of profit was gone" (Acts 16:19). They dragged Paul and Silas before the magistrates and leveled serious charges. These men are disturbing the city and promoting customs "not lawful for us Romans to adopt or practice" (v. 21). The crowd joined in, and the jailer locked them up as he was instructed. About midnight, while these prisoners were praying and singing hymns to God, an earthquake broke open the cell doors. When the jailer realized what had happened, he was going to commit suicide. Recall earlier when Peter was liberated from prison and could not be found, Herod had the guards executed (Acts 12:19). Paul intervened, acceded to the jailer's request ("what must I do to be saved?" [Acts 16:30]), then baptized him with his entire household. Once again, the response is that of a collectivistic person in a group-oriented culture. The jailer took the prisoners home and fed them, and all rejoiced at having come to faith in God.

The next day, the magistrates determined to free the prisoners, but of course, they were already free! Then Paul made a startling announcement. He revealed that they are Roman citizens who have been publicly beaten and jailed without trial. He insisted on an honorable redress. The magistrates would have to personally come to reverse their shame. The magistrates were alarmed at the news. They led the prisoners out and asked them to leave the city. The freed men returned to Lydia's house, bid farewell to the brothers, and left.

Contemporary biblical scholars agree that Acts of the Apostles is not a reliable historical source. It is, of course, based on some actual events, but Luke has reinterpreted these events to make other emphases. The question at this point is: if Paul really was a Roman citizen, why did he make no mention of it in his letters? Why did he give no clue at all to that citizenship? It is difficult to prove that Paul was a citizen of Tarsus or a Roman citizen or the independently wealthy person who did not need to work but had leisure to preach as Luke portrays him in Acts of the Apostles. The Stegemanns state quite clearly the contemporary scholarly position on Paul's status. "In our view, the Lukan picture of Paul represents a literary fiction, and for the estimation of the social position of the historical Paul, his own letters have priority. The historical Paul was a citizen of neither Rome nor Tarsus" (Stegemann and Stegemann 1999: 302).

Acts 17:1-15 Hunted in Thessalonica; welcomed in Beroea

Continuing westward along the Via Egnatia, the group arrived in Thessalonica and stayed for three Sabbaths discussing Scripture in the synagogue and demonstrating that Jesus is the Messiah. Some, including prominent women, were convinced and joined Paul and Silas. Fellow Judeans, however, became jealous. When the honor of some increases, the honor of others decreases. These opponents set the city in turmoil. Marching with a mob on the house of Jason where they thought Paul and Silas were staying, they found only Jason. So they took Jason and some believers to the magistrates and charged that they were literally "turning the world order upside down" (v. 6). Worse, the opponents charged that Paul and Silas oppose Caesar and claim that Jesus is king. The magistrates fined them and released them.

Meanwhile, the brothers sent Paul and Silas forty six and a half miles southwest to Beroea during the night. Upon arrival they went to the synagogue where the listeners diligently analyzed the Scriptures to verify Paul's message. Many, again including influential women and men, became believers. But the jealous Judeans of Thessalonica came to Beroea and once again stirred up mob opposition. Silas and Timothy remained while Paul's escorts whisked him away to Athens. Paul hoped they would soon join him there.

Acts 17:16-34 Questioned in Athens

While waiting for his associates to join him in Athens, Paul visited the synagogue as was his custom, but also debated in the public square, the agora, with any one he met there. In particular, Epicurean and Stoic philosophers engaged him. Epicureans promoted attainment of happiness through virtue and denied divine intervention in human affairs. Stoics advocated the pursuit of reason and discipline to live in harmony with nature permeated by a divine principle. They heard Paul's message as novel and strange (vv. 19-20). Was he introducing new gods: "Jesus" and his consort "Anastasia" (a misconstrual of the Greek word for resurrection)? Nevertheless, they wanted to understand these things.

The speech that Luke crafted to insert in Paul's mouth is, like all the speeches in Acts, a masterpiece. His theme represented in the words "Unknown," "unknowingly," and "ignorance" (vv. 23, 30) was a response to their suspicion that he was introducing "foreign" or "strange" notions (v. 20). Paul's focus is God, and how God ought to be properly understood. God doesn't need a temple (like the Parthenon) nor does God need anything that creatures might make. God, the one and only God, is totally in charge. The aim of the speech was to guide the listeners toward monotheism. Jesus was not mentioned by name in this speech. When Paul spoke of the man appointed for judgment and whom God raised from the dead, the audience gave its typical response. Some scoffed, others were interested in learning more, and some joined him. Two in particular who joined Paul are named: Dionysius and Damaris (a woman).

For reflection:

1. The different speeches composed by Luke for Peter and Paul and others reveal him to be a learned man, capable of tailoring the Messianist message to a variety of audiences. How would you present the message to believers in the modern world who are members of other denominations? Or to people of other religions?

2. Greek mythology speaks of a demi-god, Asclepius, who was slain and then raised from the dead by Zeus. He was a very popular god of healing in the ancient world, identified by Church Fathers as one of the biggest obstacles to faith in Jesus. Why did the educated listeners in Paul's audience scoff when they heard about "resurrection of the dead?" Did they not believe that Zeus raised Asclepius? Did they consider it "just a myth"? If so, why did they erect an altar to the "Unknown god"?

Acts 18:1-17 Reviled in Corinth

From Athens, Paul traveled to Corinth about A.D. 51 where he met Aquila and Priscilla. It is likely they became believers in Jesus the Messiah already in Rome. They migrated to Corinth because Emperor Claudius exiled all members of the house of Israel whose faith in Jesus was causing disturbances. Because they shared the same trade (tent-making), Paul stayed with them. Every week he held discussion in the synagogue hoping to persuade his listeners that the Messiah was Jesus. But since opposition remained steady, Paul decided to abandon preaching to fellow members of the house of Israel and go instead to the non-Israelites (v. 6). Yet he moved in with Titus Justus, a God-fearer, right next door to a synagogue (v. 7) and stayed quite a long time (a year and a half, v. 11). If he no longer visited the synagogue, it seems that some came to him. Eventually Crispus, the synagogue official, believed and was baptized along with his entire household (1 Cor 1:14). Many other Corinthians also believed and were baptized.

No doubt disturbed by the harassment of fellow Judeans and now living next to a synagogue, Paul could use some encouragement. It came in a night vision. The Lord spoke directly to Paul: "Do not be afraid. Go on speaking, and do not be silent, for I am with you. No one will attack you and harm you, for I have many people in this city" (Acts 18:9-10). Such encouraging visions were experienced also by ancient Israelite holy men such as Moses (Exod 3:10-15; 4:10-12), Joshua (Josh 1:1-9), and Jeremiah (Jer 1:4-10). The distinctive part of the Lord's message is that the Greek word Luke customarily uses for the people of Israel *(laos)* now includes Greeks as well all within the one people of God.

While there is no indication that Paul induced this vision, it fits the category of "divination" established by Goodman (1990: 88–99). This type of vision soothes anxiety, exposes what is hidden, and aids in decision making. It was obviously this vision that strengthened Paul to remain in Corinth for a year and a half despite fierce opposition from fellow members of the house of Israel.

Eventually the opposition resorted to the strategy already familiar in Acts. They brought him to the local magistrate and charged him with "inducing people to worship God contrary to the law" (v. 13). Gallio's response (of course, crafted by Luke) spoke more truth than he realized. Literally, he said, "It is a matter of questions about words and names and your own

Torah" (v. 14). Yes, Paul "taught the word of God" (v. 11) for eighteen months, and preached the name of Jesus Messiah (v. 5). As for Torah, Paul seems always careful to observe it himself. Before he left Cenchrae (the port of Corinth), he cut his hair in token of his Nazirite vow. According to Numbers 6:1-21, the cutting of hair grown during the period of such a vow was to take place in a Temple ritual. Since Paul cut it at Cenchrae, he might not be so Torah observant as Luke would have us believe. Clearly, Luke does not seem to know this, else he would likely not have reported it.

When Gallio dismissed the case, the frustrated crowd beat up Sosthenes, the new synagogue leader. The crowd had lost its previous synagogue leader to Paul, and now it had lost its appeal to Gallio. It was probably nothing more than frustration that can explain that beating.

Acts 18:18–19:41 Mobbed in Ephesus

From Corinth, Paul traveled with Priscilla and Aquila to Ephesus where he left them as he continued to Caesarea, likely on his way to Jerusalem ("went up" is a term that usually describes a pilgrimage to Jerusalem Acts 11:2; 15:2; 21:15; 24:11; 15:1, 9). While Paul was traveling, a Messianist, that is, a member of the house of Israel who accepted Jesus as Messiah, was teaching "the Way of the Lord" (v. 25) in Ephesus. This was Apollos, a native of Alexandria, the second largest city in the Empire and a center of intellectual and cultural activity. The city had a large museum and a four-hundred-thousand-volume library. It was here, according to a legend, that the Hebrew Scriptures were translated into Greek (the Septuagint) around 200 B.C.E. (The actual translation was probably carried out over two or three centuries.) When Priscilla and Aquila heard Apollos explaining these Greek Scriptures in the assembly, they recognized that his knowledge about Jesus was incomplete. So they explained the Scriptures privately to him "more accurately."

Since Apollos knew only the baptism of John (v. 25), he himself was likely not baptized in the name of Jesus until Priscilla and Aquila did that. Then respecting his desires, the community gave Apollos letters of recommendation for his trip to and subsequent preaching in Achaia (eventually Corinth) where he refuted fellow members of the house of Israel in public (a shaming strategy) and proved from Scripture that "the Messiah is Jesus" (v. 28).

Paul finally arrived at Ephesus and discovered some disciples who had only been baptized with John's baptism (Acts 19:1-17). They had not yet received the holy Spirit, so Paul instructed them (Acts 19:4), baptized them in the name of Jesus (v. 5), and laid his hands on them (v. 6). With this ritual rite, the holy Spirit came upon the group of twelve and they spoke with tongues and prophesied (v. 7). It is important to note that these are two different trance activities: speaking with tongues is lexically non-communicative musical sound as explained above (see comments on Acts 2); prophesying is presenting the will of God for the here and now in intelligible language (Acts 10:46; 19:6).

Goodman's seventeen years of research among glossolalists in a Yucatan village identifies this same two-fold activity, one following upon the other. "The dancers fall on their knees and there is glossolalia, loudest from Aurelia. She soon passes into intelligible speech, which then loses its trance-produced intonation and becomes a stereotyped prayer with conventional phrases. Then she returns into trance and glossolalia. She continues this alternation" (Goodman 2001: 429). Recall Paul's reflections on these matters in 1 Corinthians 14:2-3: "One who speaks in a tongue does not speak to human beings but to God. . . . One who prophesies does speak to human beings." Luke does not report what was said, so it is futile to try to determine that. All Luke intends to do here is to show the continuing infusion of the Spirit along with the Spirit's gifts into the believing community. This scene is yet another confirmation of the citation from Joel in Peter's speech (Acts 2:17-18).

For reflection:

1. Dr. Goodman's identification of an alternating pattern between trance experience and ordinary awareness as reflected also in Acts 10:46 and 19:6 confirms the scientific observation that all human beings are and for millennia have been "hardwired by God" for such experiences. If you remember, keep a record for one day of how many times your level of awareness has changed. Were any associated with prayer?

2. The sequence of believing in Jesus, being baptized in his name, and receiving the Spirit varies in Acts. Samaritan believers received the Spirit only some while after they were baptized and believed (Acts 8:14-17). Cornelius and his household received the Spirit and were then baptized! (Acts 10:44-48). The connection is important, but the Spirit cannot be tied down to a sequence. What are your experiences of the Spirit?

For three months following this event, Paul debated about the kingdom of God in the synagogue. Since his arguments fell on deaf ears and resulted in their disparaging the Way (shaming it) before the group, Paul took his disciples and for the next two years he held daily discussions about the word of the Lord in the lecture hall of Tyrannus. It is not clear whether Tyrannus is a local philosopher or the owner of the building. Be that as it may, this is a public place hence one capable of drawing a wide audience. Indeed, from this place inhabitants of Colossae, Laodicea, and Hierapolis very likely heard the message.

The summary of Paul's mighty deeds in Acts 19:11-12 describes the Paul of later legend rather than the historical Paul. Paul nowhere in his letters refers to exorcisms. Luke intends to link Paul with the activity of the Apostles in Jerusalem (Acts 5:12-16). He demonstrates that God worked extraordinary, mighty deeds through the hands of Paul the Holy Man endowed with the power of the Spirit. People are healed and evil spirits flee just by coming into contact with cloths that touched Paul. At this point seven exorcist sons of a Judaic high priest named

Sceva are introduced (Acts 19:13-20). The formula they used when addressing a person possessed by evil spirits was: "I adjure you by the Jesus whom Paul preaches" to leave this person (v. 13). The formula is part of a ritual rite, the customary means of communication with the realm of God (Goodman 1990: 55).

One evil spirit responded: "Jesus I recognize, Paul I know, but who are you?" (v. 15). Once again the text gives no explicit indication of it, yet it is plausible to assume that this dialogue with spirits, hence this exorcism ritual rite, takes place in an altered state of consciousness. Contact with beings from realm of God always takes place in an altered state of consciousness. Indeed, the spirit itself testifies to Paul's familiarity with beings in the realm of God. "Paul I know!" What is noteworthy in this exchange is that the spirit does not recognize these exorcists.

This raises a question about what sector of the realm of God (if any) these exorcists have visited? It would seem that if they did visit alternate reality, they did not find or adopt a guiding spirit in that realm. One ought not visit this realm without some instruction and some assistance from experienced facilitators in ordinary reality, such as Holy Men or Holy Women. All cultures identify such people in their midst and agree that a major characteristic of holy people is that they have direct contact with the realm of God and can mediate between that realm and ordinary reality. Moreover, experienced Holy Men and Holy Women commonly encourage those who would communicate with the realm of God to petition the spirits from that realm for assistance, to seek out a helping spirit or "guardian angel" (see Tobit 3:16-17; 5:4).

The spirits know that their reality and ordinary reality belong together as two halves of one whole. Good spirits are always willing to help human beings in ordinary reality. They just need to be invited, to be asked (Goodman 1990: 55). Perhaps these seven are just pretending to be exorcists, to be familiar with the realm of God. Perhaps they simply are mouthing formulas to impress the audience (much like Simon

Magus earlier). The evil spirit masters all seven and overpowers them, causing them to flee the house naked and wounded. This is not just a humorous touch in Luke's story. It indicates that they had little if any familiarity with the realm of God. All cultures consider such ignorance very dangerous.

Commentators usually point out, quite correctly, that Luke once again is contrasting authentic power from God with manipulative magic. What the insights from psychological anthropology on altered states of consciousness add to this picture is the human, cultural context in which to understand these experiences. In other words, commentators have too often resorted to saying that Luke was using literary devices and literary imagination to make a point. Even if these events are entirely fabricated by Luke, they have to make plausible, cultural, experiential sense in the minds of the listeners/readers. Ongoing altered states of consciousness experiences and familiarity with the realm of God and its inhabitants (alternate reality) confirm that plausibility.

The end result of this episode is that many who believed in Jesus came forward to confess that they may have been hedging: placing confidence in the power of God while being reluctant to relinquish a lingering attachment to magic. This event gave them the opportunity to choose, and they chose to trust the word of the Lord. They gathered and burned all their books, valued at a very high price. A very small notice in Acts 19:21 literally states that "Paul resolved in the Spirit to pass through Macedonia and Achaia and to go to Jerusalem. . . ." The New American Bible translates this "Paul made up his mind" in accord with the suggestion of Danker in his *Greek English Lexicon* (p. 833). Danker does point out, however, that some lexicographers would translate and interpret this phrase as pointing to the inspiration of the Spirit. We prefer this latter interpretation in line with behavior typical of collectivistic personalities in collectivistic cultures. Paul was not a Western individualist who made and kept long range plans on his own. Like others in this culture, his primary orientation to behavior is spontaneity (Pilch 1990: 87). He felt inspired by the Spirit, plausibly in an altered state of consciousness clearly not as dramatic as the Spirit's travel plans enunciated in Acts 16:6-10, to travel to Jerusalem and eventually to Rome, quite a distance from Ephesus. He tarried, however, in Ephesus for a while.

For reflection:

1. What sources might one read to learn more about alternate reality or the realm of God in the Christian tradition? Of course, a careful reading of the Bible with fresh lenses focused on this experience would be a good place to begin. What about the writings of St. Francis of Assisi, St. Bonaventure, St. Clare of Assisi, St. Agnes of Prague, St. Catherine of Siena, and other holy women and men? We have a two-thousand-year tradition just chock full of such information, a true treasure waiting to be rediscovered.

2. Paul was convinced that God set him apart and called him to be an Apostle and revealed his Son to him (Gal 1:15-16). Francis of Assisi wrote in his Testament (October, 1226): "After the Lord gave me brothers, no one showed me what I should do, but the Most High Himself revealed to me that I should live according to the form of the Holy Gospel." The sons of Sceva exhibited nothing like this confidence at all. How can one distinguish authentic from inauthentic revelation?

All scholars recognize the humorous dimension of Luke's report about the riot stirred by Demetrius and the silversmiths (Acts 19:23-40). The charges against Paul, all couched in terms of the core cultural value, "honor," are that Paul's preaching activity had "discredited" the business of silversmith souvenir makers, Artemis' temple (one of the seven wonders of the ancient world) "will be of no account," the goddess herself "will be stripped of her magnificence" (v. 27). These are three shameful outcomes of Paul's preaching. The enraged tradesmen run into the streets toward the theater shouting "Great is

Artemis of the Ephesians" (v. 28). All the city is filling the theater (25,000 seating capacity) but is totally confused (vv. 29, 32), many not even knowing why they had gathered.

Alexander, a Judean, is put forward to speak, but he is shouted down. It is not certain whether he would have spoken in support of Paul as one of those who joined him, or separated himself and fellow members of the house of Israel from this renegade (see Acts 19:9-10). The crowd continued their chant for two more hours. Finally, the town clerk silenced them, restored them to reason and good order, and dismissed the assembly. Paul who wanted to address this crowd was advised against it by friends (Asiarchs, v. 31) although his companions, Gaius and Aristarchus did not escape the crowd's wrath.

Acts 20:1–21:14 Nurturing the churches

A pattern of Paul's nurturing visits emerges in Acts 20:1: (1) he sends for disciples, (2) encourages them, and (3) bids farewell (20:1; 20:17, 36-38; 21:4-6). Indeed, Paul thinks "they would never see his face again" (Acts 20:38, see 25). In Acts 20:17-38, Paul bids farewell to the Ephesian elders. In this speech, he presents a review of his work followed by a preview. The preview elements focus on the dangers Paul and the Ephesian church face. Notice the tip-off phrases: "But now" (vv. 22, 25), and an emphatic "I know" (v. 29). The somber intuition is that they may never see his face again (Acts 20: 25, 38).

Acts 20:1-12 Back to Troas

Probably around the middle of A.D. 57, Paul traveled first to Macedonia and stayed in Greece (Corinth) for three winter months (A.D. 57–58). When opponents plotted against his life, he looped back from Philippi to Troas, which he reached after a five-day sail. Here he spent a week. The evening before he was to leave, the community gathered to break bread, and

Paul talked on and on. Eutychus, who was sitting on the window sill, sank into a deep sleep and fell from the third story to his death (v. 9). Paul went down, threw himself upon the lad (compare 1 Kgs 17:21; 2 Kgs 4:34), embraced him, and said that he lives. Returning upstairs, Paul spoke until daybreak and departed.

The story of Eutychus puts Paul in the company of Elijah, Elisha, Jesus, and Peter (Acts 9:36-43). This was, in fact, Luke's intention. But Howard takes Paul's comment seriously: "There is life in him" (2001: 215–16). Lucky for the boy, he probably suffered only a concussion and may have been unconscious. Though the crowd thought he was dead, Paul knew he was alive. There is no indication that Paul restored him to life or intended to do that.

Acts 20:13-38 Farewell to the Ephesians

As he traveled on his way to Jerusalem, Paul met with his Ephesian friends at Miletus. His speech is a genre new to Acts ("Farewell discourse") but familiar from other parts of the Bible. We have the farewells or final words of Jacob (Gen 49), Moses (Deut 31–34), Joshua (Josh 23–24), Samuel (1 Sam 12), David (1 Kgs 2:1-17), and Jesus (John 13–17; Matt 28:16-20; Luke 24:44-52). Paul's final words to the Ephesian leadership follows a pattern. He presents a review of his activity (Acts 20:18b-21), a preview of what is forthcoming (Acts 20:22-24), and a testament (Acts 20:25-31), concluding with a commendation (Acts 20:32-35).

The review of Paul's activity reveals some personal dimensions. Humility is that Mediterranean value that guides a person not to claim more for self than is deserved. Ideally, in fact, humility means intentionally putting oneself a notch below one's status so that others can acknowledge and raise a person to his or her rightful status. The Corinthian estimate that Paul's "humility" seemed to them more like timidity or obsequiousness (2 Cor 10:1) may, if true, indicate that Paul practiced this virtue very well. "Tears" (vv. 20:19, 32) can likely be interpreted literally since Mediterranean men do not hesitate to demonstrate emotion. Emotional life revolves around polarities such as shame and honor, pride and humility, burst of energetic activity and seeming lethargic passivity, and so on. Yet Paul "did not shrink" (vv. 20, 27) from presenting God's will as God revealed it to him. "But now, compelled by the Spirit, I am going to Jerusalem. What will happen to me there I do not know, except that . . . the holy Spirit has been warning me . . . ." about what awaits me (Acts 20:22-23).

This is surely a reference to on-going trance experiences in which Paul communicates with the Spirit, and the Spirit with Paul imparting knowledge of his destiny. Trance is clearly a key element in the holy man Paul's life. It is how he communicated with the realm of God on an ongoing basis. Just a few verses later Paul reminds his listeners that he hopes to finish "the ministry that I received from the Lord Jesus. . . ." (v. 24). This is surely a reference to his experience described in Acts 9 and personally reported in Galatians 1:11-12.

In the second part of his farewell speech (Acts 20:22-24), Paul presents a preview of what is imminent on the horizon. The ancients believed that a person about to die is capable of knowing what will happen to himself or herself and to persons near and dear to him or her. They have this knowledge because they are closer to the realm of God than ever before, and God knows all things. He is "compelled by the Spirit" (v. 22) to face an unknown fate, though the Spirit has indicated that he can expect imprisonment and hardships. Once again, though there is no explicit mention of a trance, it is plausible that in his prayers and meditations Paul received these insights, perhaps even verbal messages, from the Spirit. Like all holy men, once called to this vocation in a trance experience (Acts 9), Paul had ongoing trance experiences in which his relationship with the realm of God and its inhabitants continued to grow stronger (Pilch 2003a). Indeed, he expected to die and hoped that he might complete his charge "to bear witness to the gospel of God's grace" (v. 24).

Paul realized this is his last visit with these people (v. 25) so in this testament part of his speech, he gave appropriate warnings about dangers that will befall the group. After Paul's departure and eventual death, heresy will arise. Enemies from without ("savage wolves") and from "your own group" will pervert the truth. Hence, the leaders are to keep watch over themselves as well as the entire flock.

With his final words, Paul places his hope in God and God's gracious word to whom he commends the threatened Ephesian community (vv. 32-25). He exhorts them to work hard as he did to help the weak and cites a common proverb, attributing it to Jesus. "It is more blessed to give than to receive." This is fully in line with Luke's emphasis on detachment, both in the Gospel and in Acts. At the end, they repay Paul's tears in kind, weeping as they bid him farewell, realizing it is a final parting (vv. 36-38).

Acts 21:1-14 On to Jerusalem

As he continued his journey from Miletus toward Jerusalem (Acts 21:1-6), Paul landed at Tyre (Phoenicia) where he sought out some disciples and stayed with them for a week. These, "through the Spirit," advised Paul against proceeding to Jerusalem. Surely the disciples received their information and advice in trance, whether by prayer or meditation. Why did the Spirit not speak to Paul directly? Actually, the Spirit had already instructed Paul, "compelling" him to travel to Jerusalem (Acts 20:22-24). How is it that these disciples feel that the Spirit advises against continuing the trip to Jerusalem?

One aspect of group-trance experience is that the participants most assuredly visit the same place(s) in the realm of God (alternate reality), but each member of the group experiences it differently. In sharing the experiences, it is always pleasantly surprising to hear how one member's experiences help to flesh out or refine or "correct" another member's experience. As the report continues, it is evident Paul did not heed their advice but held resolutely to the inspiration he received earlier. Paul proceeded to Ptolemais, and then to Caesarea Maritima.

Paul did not establish a church at Caesarea. He had been among those who initiated the persecution that drove the witnesses out of Jerusalem, one of whom was Philip. It was Philip who had initially evangelized Caesarea (Acts 8:1-4, 40). Isn't it ironic that Paul, the former persecutor, is welcomed in the home of those who suffered as a result of his persecution, while Paul himself is on the way to persecution awaiting him in Jerusalem? Philip had four unmarried daughters "gifted with prophecy." This was not only a fulfillment of Joel's prophecy cited by Peter in his Pentecost speech (Acts 2:16-18), but it also identified holy women who, like holy men, have direct access to the realm of God and mediate gifts, in this case prophecy, to ordinary reality. Prophecy in the Bible is speaking God's will for the here and now, speaking in the name and on behalf of God. Once again, although the text does not explicitly say this, these women communicated with God in the way that is customary for holy women and holy men, namely, religious ecstatic trance, or altered states of consciousness. Unfortunately, Luke who among the Evangelists pays special attention to women, reports none of these women's prophecies. They must yield center stage to the next visitor, Agabus.

While Paul was in the house of Philip, Agabus, a prophet from Jerusalem, came and performed a symbolic action with Paul. Prophetic symbolic actions are deeds that effectively set in motion, irrevocably, the will of God. Among the classical prophets who performed such symbolic acts are Jeremiah (13:1-11) and Ezekiel (4:1–8). Agabus began by saying: "Thus says the holy Spirit" (v. 11). Agabus received his information or inspiration from the Spirit in an altered state of consciousness. He is now implementing it for and with Paul. He took Paul's cincture and bound his own hands and feet with it, saying: "This is the way the [Judeans] will bind the owner of this belt in Jerusalem, and they will hand him over to the [non-Israelites]" (Acts 21:11).

These two events are noteworthy. The disciples at Tyre, at the inspiration of the Spirit, urged Paul not to go to Jerusalem. Agabus, also speaking in the Spirit, foretold Paul's destiny there. What did the Spirit want? Discerning is always difficult. The previous storyline indicated that Paul did indeed correctly understand and interpret the will of the Spirit (see Acts 19:21; 20:22-23). There is no doubt that human emotions, normal human responses to threatening and terrifying experiences, can cloud one's vision and judgment. No doubt that is what happened to the disciples in Tyre and those in the house of Philip. Jesus himself wrestled with God's will (Luke 22:42), but ultimately declared: "Not my will but yours be done." So, too, finally, say the friends of Paul when they are convinced of his determination to even die for Jesus: "The Lord's will be done" (Acts 21:14).

For reflection:

1. How is it possible for believers (e.g., Paul and the disciples in Tyre) to give different interpretations to their inspirations from the Spirit? Could it be that the message is not dictated but only prompted and needs to be tested as well as interpreted? How is the inspiration clarified or made more precise?

2. In your experience, how does a community of believers work out differing and conflicting understandings and interpretations of the will of the Lord?

Acts 21:15-36 Evaluation in Jerusalem

In the concluding segment of this expedition (Acts 21:15-36), Paul arrived in Jerusalem and then had to deal with three groups: Mnason and the brothers (Acts 21:15-17), James and the elders (Acts 21:18-26), and the Asian members of the house of Israel and the crowd (Acts 21: 27-36). Some disciples from Caesarea accompanied Paul to the home of Mnason of Cyprus, who was an early disciple. (At this point in the Acts storyline, it is about the year A.D. 58.) The brothers welcomed Paul and his entourage. Paul was to stay with Mnason.

The next day, Paul accompanied the group to visit James and the elders (presbyters). Here Paul's reception was a bit cooler, even though they praised God at hearing of Paul's success among non-Israelites (Acts 21:19). There was concern among devout members of the house of Israel that Paul was not only not faithful to Mosaic practices but was encouraging others to abandon them. They commanded Paul ("so do what we tell you" v. 23) to demonstrate his fidelity to tradition by personally participating in and paying for four other participants in the ritual of a purity vow. Paul obeyed the very next day (v. 26).

But part of this narrative appears at odds with the meeting in Jerusalem, which it reprises. One gets the impression that Paul is learning about the decision of how to deal with non-Israelites who join the community of believers in Jesus, the Messiah (Acts 21:25), as if he had not participated in that meeting (Acts 15:12) nor disseminated its decisions (Acts 16:4). Moreover, James' report of the decision (Acts 21:25) repeats the obligations imposed on non-Israelites (Acts 15:20) but not the concern to protect their freedom (Acts 15:19, 28; compare Acts 21:28-29—non-Israelites were certainly permitted into the court of the non-Israelites). It is possible the decree promulgated around A.D. 49 evolved in understanding and application by A.D. 58-59.

It is the third group Paul met in Jerusalem that compounded his troubles: Israelites from Asia. They seized him and publicly charged him with stirring opinion against "the people and the law and this place" (v. 28) and with bringing non-Israelites into the sacred precincts of the Temple. Nothing we have read in Acts comes even close to substantiating this charge. Paul was seen with a Gentile in the city, not in the Temple. In the Temple he surely must have been seen with four fellow Israelites fulfilling a purity vow. To Paul's rescue from this mob riot came a cohort commander (leader of a thousand men) who arrested and chained him in order to ascertain what indeed Paul had done. Agabus' prophecy was fulfilled but ironically. It is not Israelites who handed Paul over to non-Israelites, but rather non-Israelite soldiers who rescued him from the Israelite mob intent on killing him. Moreover, none of the "many thousands of believers among the [Israelites]" (Acts 21:20, RSV) rescued Paul, but rather one thousand non-Israelite soldiers.

Chapter 5

Acts 21:37–28:15
Prisoner's Progress

Paul remained a prisoner for the rest of Acts, but he was in no way hampered in his ministry. He was a prisoner for several years, but according to Luke he did not languish. As a prisoner, he managed to move geographically westward through three capital cities: Jerusalem, the capital of Judea; then to Caesarea, the Roman provincial capital; and finally to Rome, the imperial capital. Spencer identifies five defense speeches before a variety of audiences and judges and two travel narratives describing his journeys between trial centers.

ACTS 21:37–23:10 TRIALS IN JERUSALEM

Paul defends himself in Jerusalem in two venues: on the steps of the prison barracks, and then before the entire high priestly council.

Acts 21:37–22:29 Paul's defense before the Jerusalem crowd

Two exchanges between Paul and the Roman tribune (Acts 21:37-40 and 22:22-29) frame his defense speech, which repeats his trance experience of the risen Jesus (22:1-21). In this entire segment Luke establishes Paul's Greek, Israelite, and Roman credentials, which render him a model witness and citizen. He is not an Egyptian (typically stereotyped as uncivilized and uneducated barbarians). Moreover, Paul speaks Greek (21:37) and Aramaic (22:2) and emphasizes his very traditional training in Jerusalem (22:3, "at the feet of Gamaliel"). We have already noted that the historical Paul was quite likely a citizen neither of Tarsus (Acts 22:3) nor of Rome as he claimed (Acts 16:37; see (Stegemann and Stegemann 1999: 302). It is also quite unlikely that he studied with Gamaliel in Jerusalem (between A.D. 20–50) since Paul never mentions this in his letters. And if he had been in Jerusalem at this time, how could he have avoided encountering Jesus? Moreover, this positive assessment of the Israelite tradition contrasts with Paul's own statements calling it "loss" and "rubbish" (Phil 3:7-8). Luke is intent on establishing Paul's ascribed and acquired honor in considerable detail.

In this report of his trance encounter with Jesus on the road to Damascus, Paul adds new information (for details, consult our comments on Acts 9). Here he identifies Jesus as "the Nazorean" (22:8) and "the Righteous One" (22:14). As for Ananias, Paul adds now that he instructed him to be baptized and wash his sins away (22:16). There is heightened emphasis in this account on what Paul saw (mention of noon; great celestial light so bright he could not see). He also changed the report about his companions' experience. Previously they heard the voice but saw no one (9:7). Now they saw the light but did not hear the voice (22:9). Finally, Paul emphasizes that he is to bear witness to what he has "seen and heard" (v. 15).

Some scholars have conducted splendid literary analyses of Paul's three reports of his encounter with Jesus in Acts (Acts 9; 22; 26; see Lohfink 1976). Such an interpretation pays credit to the literary genius of Luke who certainly knew how to craft a story to great effect. Be that as it may, the constant element in the three reports is Paul's experience of Jesus in trance. Even if Luke has fictionalized or reinterpreted that experience, the report must still make plausible cultural sense to an audience that is personally familiar with trance. Since the visual element is central to trance, it is not surprising that on the second telling, the visionary may remember more details or the experience more clearly. The visual elements are not always immediately clear, nor are they always logically or chronologically connected. The visionary must make an effort to remember what was seen immediately after the trance is ended. Those who can are urged to write down what they saw (recall in the prophetic books how often God instructs prophets in vision to "write" this or that down; Exod 17:14; 34:27; Deut 31:19; Isa 8:1; Jer 36:2; Ezek 24:2; Rev 1:11, 19; 21:2; etc.). In the writing, elements of the trance are clarified. If one later transcribes the immediate notes, the transcription is often further interpreted because one remembers more or more clearly. Recalling as already noted above that the visionary provides the sound track, it is not surprising that the dialogue portion of the three reports remain basically unchanged.

Another new element in this report is that much later after his experience, when Paul returned to Jerusalem, he was praying in the Temple and fell into a trance. Acts has reported many instances of people praying and falling into trance. For believers, prayer is not only a common context for trance but can also induce trance. Since prayer involves intense concentration, neurologically the trance is induced "from the top down" (see p. 41 above). In this instance, Jesus tells Paul to flee Jerusalem "because they will not accept your testimony about me" (Acts 22:18, RSV). Moreover, it is here in the Jerusalem Temple and not in Damascus (Acts 9:15) that Paul receives his charge to go among the non-Israelites. This is probably on Luke's part a deliberate echo of the charge Isaiah received in a Temple vision (Isa 6:1-9) that sent him to preach. He, too, doubted his abilities to be effective (like Paul, vv. 19-20) and that the people of Judah would accept his preaching (Isa 6:9-13). Jesus tells Paul the same thing: the audience in Jerusalem will not listen (v. 18). Here, too, while some scholars will see the literary hand of Luke at work, it is also plausible and highly probable that Paul, who is quite familiar with his scriptural tradition, draws upon it to interpret his own trance experience. The Israelite tradition is the latent discourse from which all visionaries in this culture will draw the interpretation of their experiences.

Lohfink (1976) thinks that these experiences served to place Paul on par with the eye-witness companions of Jesus, the Apostles. Perhaps it is more correct to say that Luke presents Paul as a prophet, especially with the allusions in Acts 22:16-18 to Ezekiel's vision (Ezek 2:1, "stand up") and Jeremiah's call ("deliver you" Jer 1:8, 19; go and speak "to whomever I send you" Jer 1:7). Luke certainly portrays Jesus as the prophet who must die in Jerusalem like prophets before him, e.g., Luke 9: 51ff.; and he draws many parallels between Jesus and Paul. This status of prophet is also how the historical Paul perceived and presented himself in his letters. His statement: "But when [God], who from my mother's womb had set me apart. . . ." (Gal 1:15) alludes to God's call of Isaiah (Is 49:1) and Jeremiah (Jer 1:4). The vision, therefore not only qualifies Paul as prophet but provides the information he needs in order to speak the will of God for the here and now like all prophets do for the house of Israel (see Acts 21:21). At the same time, Paul's on-going experiences of Jesus in ecstatic trance illustrates what the biblical tradition knows very well: ASC experiences are the customary vehicle by which God and other beings in the realm of God (alternate reality) communicate with human beings in culturally "normal" reality (see 1 Sam 3:1-21).

The fact that Paul had a vision in the Temple also refuted the charge leveled at him, that he brought non-Israelites into the Temple. On the contrary, he went there to pray. The crowd's response to Paul's self-defense was to demand his life (Acts 22:22-29)! They obviously have not been persuaded. Since the crowd was once more verging on rioting, the cohort commander determined to interrogate Paul "under the lash" to discover the reason for the crowd's hostility. After he was tied down, Paul disclosed that he was a born Roman citizen. The punishment was halted, and the cohort commander summoned the chief priests and Sanhedrin for Paul to explain himself to them.

For reflection:

1. How well do you know the biblical tradition? How might it help you to understand and interpret a dream, or vision, or some other experience in an altered state of consciousness?

Acts 22:30–23:10 Paul's defense before the Jerusalem council

When presented with an opportunity to address the Jerusalem council, Paul "stared" or "looked intently" at them. Recall our earlier discussion of this word (p. 40 above). It is possible that Paul, about to defend himself before fellow ethnics, knows how persuasive and convincing he must be. Musicians (singers, performers) sometimes go into a mild trance to enhance their performance. It is possible that Paul has done this. Or it may be that Paul "stares" at the council in an attempt through eye-contact to "enchant" them, as it were. He hopes that by joining this intense eye-contact to the words he will speak he will be able to captivate, charm, convince the listeners. The merit of this interpretation appears to be confirmed by the response from some scribes of the Pharisee party: "Suppose a spirit or an angel has spoken to him?" (Acts 23:9). This would suggest that the audience recognized that Paul was in a trance as he spoke. Paul would be receiving the benefit of the promise made by Jesus: "Remember, you are not to prepare your defense beforehand, for I myself shall give you a wisdom in speaking that all your adversaries will be powerless to resist or refute" (Luke 21:14-15).

The high priest's order to strike Paul on the mouth is certainly an intentional shaming strategy. However, since the order is given just as Paul "looked intently" at the assembly and uttered his first sentence, the gesture could be a deliberate attempt to break Paul's trance, thus reducing his effectiveness. The exchange that follows is certainly about honor. Paul accuses the high priest of violating the Torah (Lev 19:15) and curses him. When the attendants remind Paul of the man's identity, he apologizes and backs off. In Middle Eastern culture, spontaneous behavior, even emotional outbursts, are normal and expected (Pilch 1990: 87). No one ever thinks of consequences (as when Peter lashes out with the sword in the dark garden at Jesus' arrest). When someone points out the foolishness of a behavior, or restrains the miscreant, the culture requires an apology or explanation such as "I don't know what came over me" or "I don't know why I did that." When informed about the person he has cursed, Paul continues to demonstrate his dedication to Torah by citing it: "You shall not curse a ruler of your people" (Exod 22:27) and by withdrawing his spontaneous insult ("whitewashed wall" see Ezek 13:10-15).

Having cleverly set the scene for himself by declaring his Pharisaic roots ("son of Pharisees" Acts 23:6), Paul then takes attention away from himself by introducing the topic of resurrection accepted by Pharisees but denied by the Sadducees. Predictably a serious discussion follows bordering on violence. Fearful for Paul's safety, the commander removes Paul and locks him up again.

ACTS 23:11-35   PERILOUS JOURNEY FROM JERUSALEM TO CAESAREA

The very next evening the Lord stood by Paul and said, "Take courage. For just as you have borne witness to my cause in Jerusalem, so you must also bear witness at Rome" (Acts 23:11). In a night vision, Paul received encouragement from Jesus directly and learned that his mission is not yet ended. By now, the holy man Paul is so in tune with the realm of God, the visions can be brief and the message very plain. These are comforting words, but they also give added insight into what is yet to come. We mentioned in relationship to Paul's testament given to the Ephesian leaders at Miletus, that the ancients believed a person soon to die was so close to the realm of God that he or she was able to know what God knows, namely, the future (Acts 20:13-38, see p. 133 above). In this culture only God knows the future (see Mark 13:32). Yet in this vision, the risen Lord gives Paul explicit direction.

Early the next morning, about forty Israelites vowed to fast until they had killed Paul. They persuade the Sanhedrin to summon Paul again for a more thorough interrogation so that they might ambush him on the way. Paul's nephew, however, learned of the plot and relayed it to Paul, who in turn sent his nephew to report it to the commander. In his turn, the commander, Claudius Lysias, summoned an incredibly large contingent of soldiers to guarantee Paul safe passage to Felix, the governor at Caesarea. In a letter to Felix, the commander admits that he found no charge deserving death or imprisonment, only embroilment in controversial matters of Torah. Claudius also directed Paul's accusers to take their case to the governor.

ACTS 24:1–26:32 TRIALS IN CAESAREA

Paul was sent to Caesarea, which brought him still closer to Rome. In Caesarea, Paul appeared before three powerful rulers with strong Roman connections. He testified before Felix (Acts 24:1-27) but remained in prison two years. Felix was succeeded by Festus, and Paul pled his case before him, too (Acts 25:1-27). At this point, Paul appealed to Caesar, and his further journey to Rome was now assured, but before that departure he appeared before Agrippa (Acts 26:1-32).

Acts 24:1-27 Paul's defense before Felix

Tertullus' accusation speech (Acts 24:2-8) and Paul's self-defense (Acts 24:10-21) share a parallel structure. Both open with "flattery" (the technical term is *captatio benevolentiae*, an attempt to gain the favor of the judge): vv. 2-4 = v. 10. Then follows a rebuttal of accusations: vv. 5-6 = vv. 11-18. Finally an exhortation that the governor examine the evidence: v. 8 = vv. 19-21.

The high priest brought some elders to Caesarea along with a professional advocate, Tertullus, to plead the case against Paul. The flattering tributes paid to Felix are not supported by historical evidence. Actually, quite the opposite is true. A Filipino proverb, however, sheds some light: "It doesn't matter if you don't love me. Just don't shame me." This proverb reflects a typical sentiment in cultures where honor is the core cultural value. To speak the truth about Felix would shame him, so if one wants to win his favor, it is better to honor him, even if the tributes are lies.

To the point, the charges are that Paul was a "pest" who stirred dissent among Israelites "all over the world"; hence, he posed a threat to peace in the empire. Moreover, he was a ringleader of the faction known as the Nazoreans. The word "faction" is preferable to sect, since the Greek word can carry a pejorative meaning, but it describes a fringe group (faction) rather than one that has separated itself from the main body (sect). Thus, if Paul was a ringleader, he was not the faithful Pharisee he insisted he was. Then followed a bold lie charging that Paul tried to desecrate the Temple. Those who accompanied Ananias chimed in to affirm the charges.

Paul's reply also begins with moderate flattery, though "many years" (v. 17) was a bit of an exaggeration. Reference to twelve days (v. 17) marked Paul as a pilgrim, not an agitator. His visit to the Temple was for purposes of worship and not for disputation or stirring controversy. In a clever twist, he called the faction "the Way" and not "the Nazoreans," thereby associating it with *halakah*, the proper way to "walk" (the Hebrew *hlk* means to walk) so as to please God. Paul again affirmed his fidelity to the "God of our ancestors" and the Law and the Prophets. He professed faith in the resurrection of righteous and unrighteous (as in Dan 12:2). And for the first time, we learn the purpose of his visit: to bring alms and offerings "for my nation" (Acts 24:17) and to complete a vow with proper ritual. Paul believed he had been brought to trial for his professed belief in the resurrection of the dead (Acts 24:20), a hope his accusers shared with him (Acts 24:15). Paul is confident that his accusers cannot prove their charges, and Felix will be able to see that (v. 13).

Felix postponed the trial to wait for the arrival of Lysias, but he ordered that Paul be kept in custody yet be permitted some freedom. He also ordered that Paul's friends be allowed to see to Paul's needs. Meanwhile, Felix, who was "accurately informed about the Way" (Acts 24:22), came with his Israelite wife Drusilla to hear Paul speak about faith in the Messiah, Jesus. When Paul spoke about righteousness and self-restraint and future judgment, Felix became frightened and dismissed Paul until a later opportunity. What frightened Felix in Paul's message? The text gives no clue, but the three topics mentioned could make Felix more than uneasy since according to Josephus, he took another man's wife, causing her to commit adultery according to the laws of her forefathers (Exod 20:14; Deut 5:18). Meanwhile, believing Paul to be a wealthy person, he had many conversations with Paul, hoping to get a bribe. Paul never yielded. After two years (about A.D. 58–60), Porcius Festus succeeded Felix, who kept Paul in prison to curry favor with the Israelites.

Acts 25:1-27 Paul's defense before Festus

Soon after assuming rule, Festus visited Jerusalem where the chief priests and leader again tried to have Paul brought to them for trial. Once again they plotted to kill him along the way. They requested this "as a favor" (Acts 25:3), which if granted obliged them to reciprocate. Festus would appreciate that indebtedness, but he must exercise his own authority. He invited them to Caesarea instead, thus unwittingly saving Paul's life. At the hearing, Paul's accusers repeated the same groundless charges. In reply, Paul declared his innocence. He had not broken Israelite law, nor offended the Temple, nor had he committed a crime against Caesar. Confident of a more fair hearing in Rome, Paul appealed to Caesar (v. 11). Festus concurred, but before Paul left for Rome, Luke inserted a historically improbable meeting with King Agrippa. Festus used the occasion of their visit to welcome him as an opportunity to seek their advice, or rather confirmation that he has handled this case with fairness and justice.

Acts 26:1-32 Paul's defense before Agrippa

In his defense before Herod Agrippa II, Paul for a third time in Acts tells the story of his encounter with the risen Jesus in trance on the road to Damascus. On this occasion the setting for Paul's report is a very public place (25:23, "audience hall"), and the speech will have a larger audience than ever before. This Agrippa came from a line of violent men. He was the son of Agrippa I, who persecuted believers and died eaten up by worms (Acts 12:1-11, 18-23). Before him, his uncle Herod Antipas, whom Jesus labeled "that fox"(Luke 13: 32), put John the Baptist to death. Will Paul denounce this Herod Agrippa's incestuous relationship with his sister, Bernice?

Paul began, as was customary in such speeches, by flattering Agrippa (26:1-3). Next he presented himself, recounting his own solid Pharisaic background (26:4-5) and declaring his hope in the resurrection (26:6-8) for which Paul insisted he was really on trial. Then he began his third recital in Acts of his encounter in trance with the risen Jesus (26:9-21). In this account, Paul stressed the auditory elements, the instructions from Jesus. Here the soundtrack was edited, refined, and more completely understood. For the first time we learn that Jesus spoke to him in Aramaic (v. 14). The text says Hebrew but Aramaic was the Semitic language commonly spoken at this time, and scholars believe Paul spoke and understood it (Fitzmyer 1990: NJBC 79:15). Trance soundtracks will normally be heard in the language of the visionary. If the visionary is multilingual, the soundtrack can come in any of the languages known to the visionary. Contemporary research in the Cuyamungue Institute confirms this.

One researcher conversant with many languages sometimes finds the soundtrack switching from English to Latin or
Polish during the vision. In Paul's trance report, Jesus then
quoted a Greek proverb: "It is hard for you to kick against the
goad" (v. 14), common in Greek literature of the time (e.g., Eu-
ripedes, *Bacchae* 794-95). Scholars concur that in his lifetime,
Jesus spoke Aramaic and very likely a rudimentary, practical
Greek. Since Paul knew Aramaic and Greek, it would not be at
all unusual for him to hear these languages in trance. He is
providing the soundtrack. Moreover, in this report, Jesus himself gave Paul the command to preach directly (v. 16) rather
than through Ananias (9:15-16; 22:12-16). He is directly commissioned to appeal to the non-Israelites. Especially noteworthy is Jesus' statement: "I . . . appoint you as a servant and
witness of what you have seen [of me] and what you will be
shown" (Acts 26:16). Paul will continue to have further trance
experiences of Jesus. This is characteristic and normal for a
holy man in all cultures: ongoing vision experiences and contact with the realm of God. In addition, Jesus' promise to "deliver" Paul suggests that his witness will henceforth be that of
a defendant. His principal audience will be the judicial system
(see Jer 1:8).

Like most visionaries, Paul immediately obeyed his vision
(Acts 26:19). He concluded by repeating his fidelity to Moses
and the prophets and his hope for resurrection of the dead
(Acts 26:22-23). Earlier in his speech he had alluded only to a
general resurrection of the dead (26:8), linking it with restoration of the Twelve tribes. But now he alluded to Jesus, the Messiah, the first one to rise from the dead (Acts 26:22-23). Jesus'
resurrection is the beginning of the promised restoration of
God's people who now will include Israelites and non-Israelites. A key word in Paul's speech now becomes clear: light.
This tell tale characteristic of a change in level of awareness
and symbol of God's presence was for Paul brighter than the
sun (Acts 26:13), but it did not blind him as in the other accounts (Acts 9:8-9; 22:11). Then Paul used the enlightenment

gained in his vision to "open their eyes that they may turn
from darkness to light. . . ." (Acts 26:18). Finally, the risen
Jesus, the Messiah, personally will proclaim "light both to our
people and to the [non-Israelites]" (Acts 26:23).

The narrator tells us the mixed response Paul received for
his defense (Acts 26:24-31). Festus thought that Paul was mad.
This was not his judgment about Paul's visions but rather
more likely about the radical shift in Paul's life from being a
persecutor of believers in Jesus to becoming an advocate on
behalf of Jesus, seeking to enroll other followers. Paul denied
Festus' charge and turned to Agrippa for conformation.
Agrippa knew the prophets and the truths that Paul had
drawn from them. But Agrippa's reply was dismissive and
sarcastic: "You will soon persuade me to play the Christian,"
using this term with a pejorative meaning (see Pilch 1999: 100).
Paul replied by saying he prayed that sooner or later all who
hear him might become as he, a believer in Jesus the Messiah.

For reflection:

1. Sometimes people who claim to have visions report their
soundtrack in "Bible-Speak," that is, the report is a nearly verbatim recitation of words of Scripture randomly selected and
associated. As we have examined the reports of trances in this
book, and now this one emphasizing the "soundtrack" (what
Paul heard), do any of them sound like "Bible-Speak"? How
does one integrate the tradition in such a way that it lends itself to interpretation without being directly quoted in the report of the vision?

2. The word "Christian" appears only three times in the
New Testament. Followers of Jesus never described themselves with this word. Luke says that they preferred to be
known as followers of "the Way" (Acts 9:2; 19:9; 22:4; 24:22).
Only outsiders use the word "Christian" (Acts 11:26; 26:28; 1
Pet 4:16-17) in mocking or pejorative fashion. Historically the
word is most appropriately used after the time of Constantine

(around A.D. 300). Prior to that time, the word is anachronistic. From this point of view, there are no "Christians" in the New Testament. How can one interpret or explain this statement?

ACTS 27:1–28:15 PERILOUS JOURNEY FROM CAESAREA TO ROME

Scholars in general agree that Luke has fashioned this story of Paul's voyage to Rome after a popular genre in the ancient world, namely, sea-voyage literature. This genre is in the tradition of such literature as the *Odyssey* and the *Aeneid*. Most scholars, in fact, believe that Luke took a pre-existing tale and inserted Paul into it at four points to highlight Paul as a holy man, a man of God. This journey was taken against the advice of the holy man, Paul (Acts 27:9), at a most inauspicious season. Autumn (late September or early October, the "time of fast" i.e., the day of atonement, see Leviticus 16:29-31) led into the period of winter storms on the Mediterranean (October to March).

Paul's warning, of course, fell on deaf ears. More than this, the plausibility of one who was a prisoner intervening and being listened to by his captors was highly unlikely! This is the first Lukan insertion of Paul, which demonstrates that he was like other well-known holy men in the Hellenistic tradition, such as Apollonius of Tyana (Philostratus, *Life of Apol* 5.18). A holy man has ready access to the realm of God and shares knowledge that only God possesses. In the storyline, the centurion, the ship owner, and the pilot ignored Paul's wisdom to everyone's peril.

Predictably in the storyline, the travelers, who included other prisoners besides Paul, experience storms (Acts 27:9-38) and eventually shipwreck (Acts 27:40). In the midst of this difficult journey, Paul received a message in a night-time trance from an angel of God: "Do not be afraid, Paul. You are destined to stand before Caesar; and behold, for your sake, God has granted safety to all who are sailing with you" (Acts 27:24). In other words, no lives will be lost, and the ship will reach its destination. God is totally in charge, and God's plan will be realized. Nothing can thwart it. This is Luke's second insertion into the travel journey.

Often in trance, the person initially does not recognize the one she or he is seeing. The one appearing calms the visionary: "Fear not!" and then identifies self: "It is I!" In Acts it seems quite clear that all the visionaries are quite familiar with the realm of God and its many inhabitants. Often, the being from the realm of God does not have to calm the fears of the visionary. In this instance, Paul recognizes his messenger: "an angel of the God to whom [I] belong and whom I serve" (Acts 27:23). Paul was not afraid because this was very likely his spirit guide from the realm of God (see p. 128 above). Just as Tobit had a guardian angel who communicates from the realm of God, so, too, does Paul.

As the storm worsened and the ship's situation became more precarious, the sailors attempted to mutiny, but the prescient holy man, Paul, once again came to the rescue of all 276 passengers on the ship. This third insertion is quickly followed by a fourth. Having been unable to eat for two weeks because of sea sickness, Paul now urged them to eat. He is presented as somehow knowing, guessing, or hoping that this time the food would "stay down." Specifically, of course, Paul broke bread with them (with intentional eucharistic overtones). This indeed will help them survive, or literally "this will be for your salvation" (v. 34, author's translation). It was immediately effective since the captain forbade the soldiers from killing the prisoners to prevent their possible escape (vv. 42-43).

The shipwrecked passengers swam onto the island of Malta (Acts 28:1-6), where the natives extended extraordinary hospitality. Paul gathered some sticks to put on the fire. A viper emerged from the fire and fastened on Paul's hand, but Paul was not at all harmed. The witnesses then made two responses. The first response was that this prisoner who survived shipwreck with his life surely had to be guilty, a murderer. The goddess Justice was now giving him his just desserts. But when after a long time Paul suffered no ill effects, indeed, he didn't die, they concluded that he had to be a god. For Luke's readers, that is, those who believed in Jesus, the Messiah, Paul was not a god at all, but a man of God, a holy man. He was the beneficiary of Jesus' promise: "I have observed Satan fall like lightning from the sky. Behold, I have given you the power 'to tread upon serpents' and scorpions and upon the full force of the enemy and nothing will harm you" (Luke 10:18-19). Howard (2001: 216–217) observes that one need not consider this a legend for there is nothing "intrinsically improbable" about it. The famed "Lawrence of Arabia" (T. E. Lawrence) reported a similar story, though there are no poisonous snakes on Malta today.

There is no indication in the text, but it is possible that if this is a factual report, Paul had slipped into trance. He may have been intensely focused on some idea, or perhaps he became entranced by staring at the flames. As we noted above (p. 53), Rouget (1985: 13–14) observed that a person in trance can "handle poisonous snakes without being bitten," and by extension not suffer the ill effects of a snake-bite.

Significantly, after this experience with the viper, Paul healed a man suffering from fever and dysentery, and many other people also (Acts 28:8-9). Howard (2001: 217–18) believes the description of Publius' father's problem (fever and dysentery) corresponds well with a response to a food-borne bacterial enterotoxin rather than a food-borne infection. An enterotoxin is a microorganism that produces gastrointestinal problems. The problem is self-limiting and usually doesn't last beyond twenty-four to forty-eight hours. Paul's response (personal visit, prayer, laying on of hands) was certainly comforting but quite likely not "miraculous." That is also probably Luke's intention as well.

On this island Paul did no preaching, but he demonstrated what the culture would identify as "mighty deeds." These and the healing of the others could well have been effected by Paul in trance. It is quite plausible and likely that Paul entered in and out of trance frequently in the course of a normal day which is a common human experience at all times and in all cultures (Clottes and Lewis-Williams 1996: 12). After a three-month stay on Malta, they set sail for Italy, landing at Puteoli, modern Puzzuoli on the Gulf of Naples.

For reflection:

1. Perhaps you have heard about contemporary Christian snake-handling congregations. Where could you learn more about them, and how would you explain their experiences? Would it be possible that these are holy people inheriting the promise of Jesus?

2. Modern western medicine knows of many self-limiting illness episodes. What impact does this knowledge such as the suggestion concerning Publius' father's problem have on the interpretation made by the witnesses or that intended by Luke?

ACTS 28:16-31 THE JOURNEY CONCLUDES

Paul finally arrived in Rome, was kept under house arrest, and met with people there over a period of two years. First Paul summoned the Israelite leaders to himself and once more declares that he has done nothing "against our people or our ancestral customs" (v. 17). He continued to identify himself as a faithful and observant member of the house of Israel. Even when turned in to Roman jurisdiction by his own people, he made "no accusation against my own nation" (v. 19). His troubles stemmed from his understanding of and preaching about "the hope of Israel," that is, the genuine source of Israel's renewal. His audiences agreed. They had received no official complaints about Paul, but they were interested in hearing more from Paul personally. He spent a day of intense reflection with them, encountering the same responses as heretofore: some were convinced while others did not believe.

But, the non-believers pursued their disagreements with the believers and didn't attack Paul, which has happened so often in earlier such contexts.

For his part, Paul delivers a parting shot which also turns out to form an *inclusio* with the beginning of Luke's Gospel (Pilch 2000: 114–16). Luke encased his two volumes (Gospel and Acts) in quotations from Isaiah. These quotations form an *inclusio*, signaling that Luke intended both books to be read as a unit. (An *inclusio* is a literary device in which an author repeats words, phrases, or ideas from the beginning of his composition at the end, signaling an intention to construct a unit.) More than that, though, the structure of these two quotations gives the reader a clue about Luke's intended message (Pilch 1999: 72-78).

In Luke 4:18–19, Jesus reads from Isaiah 61:1-2:

> A bring good news to the poor
>   B release to the captives/debtors
>   C SIGHT TO THE BLIND
>   B' release to the oppressed
> A' announce a year of favor from the Lord.

The concentric arrangement singles out blindness which is a significant concern in Luke's works (see Luke 4:18; 6:39; 7:21-22; 11:34-36; 18:35-43; Acts 9:18; 22:13; 13:11). While these apparently are references to physical blindness, there are many references to socio-cultural blindness or lack of understanding, and to seeing or understanding: a parable about judging (6:39-42); a parable of the sower (8:9-16), a parable of the lamp (16-18); a makarism (more appropriate word for "beatitude") on seeing (10:21-24); the sign of Jonah (11:29-32); a parable on the lamp (33-36); signs on the earth and in the sky (12:54-56); yearning to "see" the Son of Man's day (17:22, 30); Herod hopes to see a sign (23:8); crowds saw and beat their breasts (23:48); you are witnesses (24:48).

Acts continues the theme of "you will be my witnesses" (1:8) and dwells on this theme of witness in the reports about Peter, Stephen, Philip, and Paul. In Acts, even though the physical blindness of some was remedied—Paul (9:18; 22:13) and Elymas (13:11)—others such as Paul's Judaic visitors (28:25) chose to remain blind by their refusal to understand the eloquent speeches of the preachers.

Indeed, the concluding verses of Acts (28:26-27) find Paul citing Isaiah 6:9-10 to describe these very people who came to listen to Paul's teaching but failed to be persuaded. Paul's Isaiah quote can be structured in this way:

> Go to this people, and say:
> A You shall indeed hear but never understand
>   B and you shall indeed see but never perceive
>   B for this people's heart has grown dull
> A and their ears are heavy of hearing
>   B and their eyes they have closed
>   B lest they should perceive with their eyes
> A and hear with their ears
>   B and understand with their heart
>   B and turn to me to heal them.

Of the three symbolic body zones (A = mouth-ears; B = heart-eyes; C = hands-feet) identified by our ancestors in faith on the human body throughout the Bible (see Pilch 2000: 106–11), this passage focuses on mouth-ears (or self-expressive speech, A) and heart-eyes (or emotion-fused though, B). Zone C, the symbolic body zone represented by "hands-feet" (the zone of purposeful action) is entirely lacking. The many reports in Acts of trance experiences help give a new interpretation to Paul's concluding quote from Isaiah. As we have noted, modern ethnography tells us that more than 90% of the planet's population readily experiences altered states of consciousness. The biblical evidence, Acts included, indicates that no one doubts or denies reports of trances that people have. It is an experience that is available to all in circum-Mediterranean culture. But, as is clear in Acts, those who oppose Paul are also opposed to Jesus, God's anointed. They thus deliberately thwart any possibility of encountering God or Jesus in an altered state of consciousness. Because it is deliberate, it is all the more lamentable. Would that modern believers would never resist encountering the living God in whatever form the Deity chooses, particularly one for which the human physical body has been magnificently prepared by the Creator.

Paul remained under house arrest for two years and spoke with all (presumably Israelites as well as non-Israelites) who came to hear him proclaim boldly and unhindered the kingdom of God and about the Lord Jesus, the Messiah. Having begun around the year A.D. 30, the storyline of Acts concludes around the year A.D. 64–67 during which period believers encountered God and beings from the realm of God in ecstatic trance experiences. Indeed, some were even healed by means of such experiences.

Conclusion

According to Gallup polls (1989: 162–64), Americans admit to having a religious experience [about 33%], are very conscious of the presence of God [81%], or have felt influenced by a presence or power including God [43%]. Subsequent studies that have replicated the Gallup probings have generally produced results with the same percentages. Thus, at least some Americans should be able to read with appreciation Luke's reports of trance experiences of the realm of God by early believers such as Peter, John, Stephen, Philip and his daughters, Paul, Ananias, Agabus, among others.

Early in the existence of the Jesus movement, these experiences were discouraged and perhaps extinguished because of the Gnostics. These latter used their singular type experiences, that is, their personal trance experiences to establish their own authority over and against apostolic claims such as those recorded in Acts. To eliminate these claims, yet to maintain the letters of Paul and the book of Revelation to which singular type, that is, personal trance experiences, contributed, apostolic authority established a canon or norm of Scripture for Jesus groups. From that time forward no other visions of Jesus had any significance for the community, especially when their message deviated from the content of the New Testament canon (Malina and Pilch 1998: 283).

The experiences, of course, persisted and were reported in the writing of the Fathers of the Church as well as in the Mystical tradition up until the next major effort to discredit them that resulted from the Enlightenment. Yet since the human person has been neurologically "hard-wired" for this experience, as contemporary brain research points out, the experience will continue as it ever has. This book invites believers to explore ways in which to restore these dimensions of the faith tradition as boldly reported by Luke.

Resource Bibliography

Chrisman, Noel
1990 "Culture Shock in the Operating Room." *Journal of Transcultural Nursing* 1: 33–39.

Clottes, Jean, and David Lewis-Williams
1996 *The Shamans of Prehistory: Trance and Magic in the Painted Caves*. Text by Jean Clottes, trans. from the French by Sophie Hawkes. New York: Harry N. Abrams, Inc.

Collins, John N.
1992 *Are all Christians Ministers*? Collegeville: Liturgical Press.

d'Aquili, Eugene G., Charles D. Laughlin, Jr., John McManus et al.
1979 *The Spectrum of Ritual: A Biogenetic Structural Analysis*. New York: Columbia University Press.

d'Aquili, Eugene G., and Andrew B. Newberg
1993 "Liminality, Trance, and Unitary States in Ritual and Meditation," *Studia Liturgica* 23 (1993) 2–34.
1999 *The Mystical Mind: Probing the Biology of Religious Experience*. Minneapolis: Fortress Press.

Dodd, C. H.
1957 "The Appearances of the Risen Christ: An Essay in Form-Criticism of the Gospels." Pp. 9-35 in *Studies in the Gospel*. Oxford: Blackwell.

Duling, Dennis
2001 "Recruitment to the Jesus Movement in Social-Scientific Perspective." Pp. 132–75 in *Social Scientific Models for Interpreting the Bible: Essays by the Context Group in Honor of Bruce J. Malina*. John J. Pilch (ed.). Leiden: E. J. Brill.

2002 "The Jesus Movement and Network Analysis." Pp. 301–32 in *The Social Setting of Jesus and the Gospels.* Wolfgang Stegemann, Bruce J. Malina, Gerd Theissen (eds). Minneapolis: Fortress.

Elliott, John H.
1991 "Temple versus Household in Luke-Acts: A Contrast in Social Institutions." Pp. 211–40 in *The Social World of Luke-Acts: Models for Interpretation.* Jerome H. Neyrey (ed.). Peabody, Mass: Hendrickson.

Esler, Philip
1987 *Community and Gospel in Luke-Acts.* Cambridge: University Press.
1992 "Glossolalia and the Admission of Gentiles into the Early Christian Community," *BTB* 22 (1992) 136–42.

Gallup, George, Jr. and Sarah Jones.
1989 *100 Questions and Answers: Religion in America.* Princeton, N.J.: Princeton Religious Research Center.

Goldman, Mark S.
1999 "Expectancy Operation: Cognitive-Neural Models and Architectures." Pp. 41-63 in Kirsch.

Goodman, Felicitas D.
1972 *Speaking in Tongues: A Cross-cultural Study of Glossolalia.* Chicago: University of Chicago Press.
1973 "Glossolalia and Hallucination in Pentecostal Congregations." *Psychiatria Clinica* 6: 97–103.
1980 "Triggering of Altered States of Consciousness as Group Event: A New Case from Yucatan." *Confinia Psychiatrica* 23:26–34.
1990 *Where the Spirits Ride the Wind: Trance Journeys and Other Ecstatic Experiences.* Bloomington, Ind.: Indiana University Press.
1997 *My Last Forty Days: A Visionary Journey among the Pueblo Spirits.* Bloomington and Indianapolis, Ind: Indiana University Press.
2001 *Maya Apocalypse: Seventeen Years with the Women of a Yucatan Village.* Bloomington and Indianapolis, Ind.: Indiana University Press.

Goodman, Felicitas D., Jeannette H. Henny, and Esther Pressel
1974 *Trance, healing, and hallucination: Three field studies in religious experience.* New York: Wiley.

Gore, Belinda.
1995 *Ecstatic Body Postures: An Alternate Reality Workbook.* Santa Fe, N.M.: Bear & Company, Inc.

Hagedorn, Anselm C., and Jerome H. Neyrey
1998 "'It was out of envy that they handed Jesus over' (Mark 15.10): The Anatomy of Envy and the Gospel of Mark." *Journal for the Study of the New Testament* 69:15–56.

Jungmann, Joseph A., S.J.
1955 *The Mass of the Roman Rite: Its Origins and Development (Missarum Solemnia).* Vol. Two. New York: Benziger Brothers, Inc.

Kinsbourne, Marcel
1998 "Unity and diversity in the brain: Evidence from injury," *Daedalus* 127: 233–56.

Kirsch, Irving (ed.)
1999 *How Expectancies Shape Experience.* Washington, D.C.: American Psychological Association.

Kottak, Conrad Philip
1978 "Rituals at McDonald's." *Natural History* 87: 74–83.

Krippner, Stanley
1972 "Altered States of Consciousness." Pp. 1–5 in *The Highest State of Consciousness.* J. White (ed). New York: Doubleday.

Lewis-Williams, David
2002 *The Mind in the Cave: Consciousness and the Origins of Art.* London: Thames & Hudson, Ltd.

Lohfink, Gerhard
1976 *The conversion of St. Paul: narrative and history in Acts.* Trans. and edited by Bruce J. Malina. Chicago: Franciscan Herald Press.

Malina, Bruce J.
1986 *Christian Origins and Cultural Anthropology: Practical Models for Biblical Interpretation.* Atlanta: John Knox.
1999 "Assessing the Historicity of Jesus' Walking on the Sea: Insights from Cross-Cultural Social Psychology." Pp. 351–71 in *Authenticating the Activities of Jesus.* New Testament Tools and Studies 28.3. Craig A. Evans and Bruce Chilton, (eds.) Leiden: Brill, 1999.

Malina, Bruce J., and John J. Pilch
2000 *Social Science Commentary on Revelation*. Minneapolis: Fortress.
2006 *Social Science Commentary on the Letters of Paul*. Minneapolis: Fortress (forthcoming).

Malina, Bruce J., and Richard L. Rohrbaugh
1998 *Social Science Commentary on the Gospel of John*. Minneapolis: Fortress.

Mol, Hans
1976 *Identity and the Sacred*. New York: The Free Press.

Murphy, G. Ronald, S.J.
1979 "A Ceremonial Ritual: The Mass." Pp. 318–41 in *The Spectrum of Ritual: A Biogenetic Structural Analysis*. Eugene d'Aquili, Laughlin, Jr., McManus, et. al. New York: Columbia University Press.

Newberg, Andrew, Eugene d'Aquili, and Vince Rouse
2001 *Why God Won't Go Away*. New York: Ballantine Books.

Neyrey, Jerome H. (ed.)
1991 *The Social World of Luke-Acts: Models for Interpretation*. Peabody, Mass: Hendrickson.

Pilch, John J.
1990 "Marian Devotion and Wellness Spirituality." *BTB* 20: 76–94.
1993 "Visions in Revelation and Alternate Consciousness: A Perspective from Cultural Anthropology." *Listening: Journal of Religion and Culture* 28: 31–244.
1994 "The Transfiguration of Jesus: An Experience of Alternate Reality." Pp. 47–64 in *Modelling Early Christianity: Social Scientific Studies of the New Testament in its Context*. Philip F. Esler (ed). London and New York: Routledge.
1996 "Altered States of Consciousness: A 'Kitbashed' Model." *BTB* 26: 133–38.
1998 "Appearances of the Risen Jesus in Cultural Context: Experiences of Alternate Reality." *BTB* 28: 52–60.
1998 "A Window into the Biblical World: Walking on the Sea," *The Bible Today* 36. 117–23.
1999 *The Cultural Dictionary of the Bible*. Collegeville: Liturgical Press.
2000 *Healing in the New Testament: Insights from Medical and Mediterranean Anthropology*. Minneapolis: Fortress Press.

2002a "Altered States of Consciousness Events in the Synoptics." In *The Social Setting of Jesus and the Gospels*. Bruce J. Malina, Wolfgang Stegemann, Gerd Theissen (eds.). Minneapolis: Fortress Press. Pp. 103–15.

2002b "The Nose and Altered States of Consciousness: Tascodrugites and Ezekiel." *Hervormde Teologiese Studies* 58: 708–20.

2002c "Paul's Ecstatic Trance Experience near Damascus in Acts of the Apostles." *Hervormde Teologiese Studies* 58: 690–707.

2003a "Becoming Holy Women and Holy Men in the New Testament." *Landas* 17: 81–91.

2003b "How We Redress Our Suffering: An Exercise in Actualizing Biblical Texts." *The Polish Review* 48: 21–42.

Pilch, John J. (ed.)
2001 *Social Scientific Models for Interpreting the Bible: Essays by the Context Group in Honor of Bruce J. Malina*. Leiden: E.J. Brill.

Quispel, G.
1998 "The Asclepius: From the Hermetic Lodge in Alexandria to the Greek Eucharist and the Roman Mass." Pp. 69–77 in *Gnosis and Hermeticism from Antiquity to Modern Times*. Roelof van den Broek and Wouter J. Hanegraaff (eds.). New York: State University of New York Press.

Rohrbaugh, Richard L.
2001 "Gossip in the New Testament." Pp. 239–59 in *Social Scientific Models for Interpreting the Bible. Essays by the Context Group in Honor of Bruce J. Malina*. John J. Pilch (ed.). Leiden, the Netherlands: E. J. Brill.

Rossi, Ernest Lawrence
1986 "Altered States of Consciousness in Everyday Life: The Ultradian Rhythms." Pp. 97–132 in *Handbook of States of Consciousness*. Benjamin B. Wolman and Montague Ullman (eds). New York: Van Nostrand Reinhold Co.

Rouget, Gilbert
1985 *Music and Trance: A Theory of the Relations between Music and Possession*. Trans. and revised in collaboration with the author by Brunhilde Biebuyck. Chicago and London: University of Chicago Press.

Spees, Everett K.
2002 "Therapeutic Storytelling with Children and Adolescents." *Encyclopedia of Psychotherapy* 2: 793–801.

Spencer, F. Scott
1997 *Acts*. Sheffield, U.K.: Academic Press.

Stegemann, Ekkehard W., and Wolfgang Stegemann.
1999 *The Jesus Movement: A Social History of its First Century.* Minneapolis: Fortress.

Strelan, Rick
2000 "Recognizing the Gods (Acts 14: 8-10)," *New Testament Studies* 46: 488–503.

Van der Horst, P. W.
1976 "Peter's Shadow. The Religio-Historical Background of Acts V.15." *New Testament Studies* 23: 204–12.

Werntz, D., R. Bickford, F. Bloom, and S. Singh-Khulsa.
1982 "Alternating cerebral hemispheric activity and lateralization of autonomic nervous function." *Neurobiology* 4: 225–29.

Winkelman, Michael
1997 "Altered States of Consciousness and Religious Behavior." Pp. 393–428 in *Anthropology of Religion*. Stephen D. Glazier, ed. London and Westport, Conn.: Praeger.
1982 "Magic: A Theoretical Reassessment," *Current Anthropology* 23: 37–66. See especially the response by Felicitas Goodman, p. 47.

Appendix 1

Outline of Acts

This outline is substantially that proposed by F. Scott Spencer, *Acts* (Sheffield: Academic Press, 1997; new edition: Peabody, MA: Hendrickson Publishers, 2004.) whose book served as a general guide to the literary analysis of Acts. I have made minor modifications to it. Because Spencer's work incorporated basic insights from the published research of The Context Group of which I am a founding member, it was a good basis on which to build this selective commentary. I was able to deepen some of his insights and add still other reflections from my own research on healing and altered states of consciousness in antiquity.

Chapter 1
Acts 1–2 The Journey Begins: Communal Religious Trance Experiences (ASCS)

Acts 1:1-26 Ascension
> Acts 1:1-11 Group trance experience of the Risen Jesus' ascension
> Acts 1:12-26 Replacing Judas

Acts 2:1-47 Pentecost
> Acts 2:1-13 Outpouring of the Spirit
>> Acts 2:1-4 Group trance experience of descent of the Spirit
>> Acts 2:5-13 Group trance experience of glossolalia

Chapter 4
Acts 13:1–21:36 Journeys into Non-Israelite Territory

Chapter 5
Acts 21:37–28:15 Prisoner's Progress

Acts 21:37–23:10 Trials in Jerusalem
Acts 21:32–22:29 Paul's defense before the Jerusalem crowd
Acts 22:30–23:10 Paul's defense before the Jerusalem Council

Acts 23:11-35 Perilous Journey from Jerusalem to Caesarea

Acts 24:1–26:32 Trials in Caesarea
Acts 24:1-27 Paul's defense before Felix
Acts 25:1-27 Paul's defense before Festus
Acts 26:1-32 Paul's defense before Agrippa

Acts 27:1–28: 15 Perilous Journey from Caesarea to Rome

Acts 28:16-31 The Journey Concludes

Appendix 2

Rite and Trance

Humans beings around the planet spend most of their waking day in what we have called ordinary, or culturally "normal," or consensual reality. This is that aspect or dimension of reality of which a person is most commonly aware most of the time. However, at various irregular or regular intervals, a large number of persons experience alternate, or non-ordinary, or non-consensual reality. This is that dimension of reality in which God or the spirits are to be found. Those periods during which persons experience alternate reality during the course of their daily life are much like time-outs in some well-organized and patterned sporting events.

Notice that baseball, football, hockey, soccer, and basketball are well organized and patterned according to the rules of the game. However, in each of these games there are time-outs, some regular and some irregular. During a time-out the flow of the game is interrupted, the line separating time-in, when every movement, gesture, and shot is significant, is halted by a metaphorical crossing of that timeline in a time-out realm. Thus during the course of any game there are various occasions for crossing from the time-in sphere into a time-out realm: (1) either because a player or group of players is hurt, dazed, confused; or (2) for the sake of substitution, when some player is ready to take the place of another in a new role; or (3) in order to mark the regular flow of the game, such as quarters or half-times so that all players get the opportunity to rest and evaluate their play. In all instances of time-outs, whether irregular, such as for hurt players or for substitutions, or regular, such as quarter and half-time breaks, the normal flow of interaction in the game comes to a halt and players move to a different social realm (see Malina 1986: 139–53).

If we consider experiences in altered or alternate states of consciousness (ASC) as time-outs in the course of living within consensual or "normal" reality, we find regular and irregular ASC experiences. Social scientists call behavior dealing with social line crossings a "rite." Since an ASC experience deals with moving across the metaphorical boundary separating the "time-in" dimension of "normal" reality from the "time-out" reality of alternate reality, such a transition entails a rite.

Rites are divided into rituals and ceremonies. Rituals are irregular time-outs. Just as irregular time-outs in a game are determined by situations or conditions that affect individual players or groups of players and cannot be predicted ahead of time except statistically, so, too, rituals occur when situations or conditions occur that unexpectedly displace affected individuals or groups into alternate reality. Consider Luke's description of Stephen's vision or of Paul's surprising experience on the road to Damascus. The pattern of behavior involved is a ritual well known in Israelite society for altered states that befall a person. Stephen "gazes," "stares," or "looks up" intently to the sky (Acts 7:55). This activity changes a person's level of awareness, puts him or her into an altered state of consciousness. Neuroscience describes it as sensory concentration so intense as to overstimulate that sense and induce trance. Paul was "breathing murderous threats against the disciples of the Lord" (Acts 9:1). He intensely focused on these people, concentrating so single-mindedly that they consumed him. Again, neuroscience describes this as mental concentration so intense that it induces a change in level of awareness, an altered state of consciousness.

Ceremonies, on the other hand, are regular time-outs. In a game, these time-outs are called for by the very structure or pattern of the game, irrespective of the condition of the players (e.g., half-time, quarter-time). In social life, ceremonies are regular rites called for by the very social structure of a group, irrespective of the wishes of the players. Wedding anniversaries, Thanksgiving day meals, Sunday worship happen quite regularly whether people wish to take note of them or not. So, too, ASC ceremonies take place at regularly scheduled and/or predicted intervals, for example, at fixed prayer times, and historically, at Sunday liturgy. In other words, there are two kinds of ASC rites: ritual ASCs that befall individuals or groups in the course of "normal" daily activity, and ceremonial ASCs that occur at predetermined times and places as required by the social structure which sets the regular rules of the life of the group.

During the course of this commentary, I have mentioned that ASC experiences follow a certain pattern, and that one or another trance experience seems to occur in the context of a rite. For example, relative to the group trance experience of Jesus' ascension, it was mentioned that certain distinctive postures assisted in inducing an altered state of awareness (Acts 1:1-11, see pp. 14–23 above). The body requires a specific tuning or orientation in order to experience alternate reality; thus, posture is essential to the rite. In addition, healing events in general in antiquity but specifically in Acts of the Apostles (by Peter and John in Acts 3:1-10, see pp. 39–43 above; and by Paul in Acts 14:1-20, see pp. 109–112 above, and in Acts 19:11-12, see p. 127 above) take place in a rite of which trance is sometimes an element explicitly mentioned. To appreciate the relationship of rite and trance, it would helpful to reflect on rite.

Mol (1976: 233) defined rite as "the repetitive enactment of human systems of meaning." The repetitive behavior pattern of both ritual and ceremonial rites are quite likely familiar to all readers. Indeed, d'Aquili and Newberg (1993: 28; 2000: 89) identify four elements in rite. Such behavior is (1) structured or patterned, that is, it is always the same. One does not invent a rite anew each time, or modify it at will. Ceremonial and ritual behavior are also (2) rhythmic and repetitive. Rhythmicity and repetition are especially conducive to inducing changes in the nervous system which is where trance originates. The regularity and even the tempo of the rite (whether it is "slow" like the Roman Catholic Liturgy of the Eucharist, or "fast" like the rite used by the Umbanda of Brazil or Sufi dancing) affects the kind of trance produced, though the trance experience will be brief yet intense. In her research and experiments, Dr. Goodman discovered that shaking a rattle about 200 to 210 beats per minute for a fifteen minute period is the optimal rhythmicity for inducing a trance (Goodman 1990: 225).

One of the effects of ceremonial and ritual behavior is that they (3) synchronize a person's affective, perceptual-cognitive, and motor processes which in turn generate powerful unifying experiences within the *individual*. Finally, (4) ceremonial rites also synchronize these same processes among members of a group thus creating a strong *sense of group unity*. We shall return to this latter characteristic of rite when we reflect on the Liturgy of the Roman Rite below.

By itself, a rite is a neutral strategy or technique which occurs in settings as diverse as McDonald's (Kottak 1978) and the operating room (Chrisman 1990). The level of trance produced in both these settings may be very light, perhaps nothing more than unreflexive behavior of learned habits similar to road trance. Many drivers admit to arriving at a destination having observed all the laws, speed limits, and the like but with no recollection of the actual journey. So, too, the rite at McDonald's or in the operating room is a learned behavior, the way it's done, and it is carried out without consciously thinking about it.

The second element in Mol's definition, that is, the connection of rite with human systems of meaning is perhaps less familiar. Rites, whether ceremonial or ritual, are a form of symbolic action, an acted out symbol, which has to do with

transitions from point A to point B across some socially defined line through time and/or space. The line crossing can be
either to a new structure (as in certain rituals) or within a
structure (as in ceremonies). Marriage, ordination, and baptism in the name of Jesus (e.g., Acts 2:38) are rituals of status
transformation marking transitions to a new structure: from
the unmarried to the married state; from the status of lay person to that of cleric; from being in Israel to being in Christ.
Healing in the name of Jesus is a ritual of status restoration, by
which a person passes from exclusion due to loss of social status to status restoration within his/her society. The celebration
of the Lord's supper, on the other hand, is a ceremony within
the Jesus group gathering, the Church.

It is significant that Jesus prescribed no rites, perhaps because essentially he was leading a Galilean reform movement,
a lifestyle of reform within Judaism. Thus, at one point he suggested selling all and following him (Luke 18:22). On another
occasion he recommended self-denial, taking up one's cross
and following him (Matt 16:24). On still another occasion,
when a would-be follower asked leave to bury his father, Jesus
told him to let the dead bury the dead and follow him forthwith (Matt 8:22). Of course, in his own healing and exorcism
activities, Jesus did follow cultural rites involving words and
gestures.

Scholars recognize that the healing activities of Peter and
John (Acts 3:1-10) and Paul (Acts 14:1-20; 19:11-12) resemble the
healing activities of Jesus (e.g., John 9, Sabbath healing of a
man born blind). Medical anthropologists identify these as examples of symbolic healing, that is, real outcomes effected by
cultural values and beliefs (Pilch 2000: 32-34, 131-138). This
symbolic healing rite contains four elements. First the healer
builds a symbolic bridge between the sick person's experience,
social relations, and cultural meanings. The lame man extended his hand to seek alms, but Peter took his right hand and
raised him up (Acts 3:1-2). Second, the healer relates the sick
person to the mythic world. Everyone in Jerusalem knew of

Jesus' crucifixion (Luke 24:18) and undoubtedly heard the reports that his tomb was empty and that he was seen alive by his followers. Peter connects the sick person's problem with this "Jesus Christ the Nazorean" now raised by God from the dead (Acts 3:6). The God who acted favorably toward Jesus can act equally favorably toward this lame man. Third, the healer uses transactional symbols (in this case, taking him by the hand and physically raising him to his feet, Acts 3:7). Finally, the healer offers confirmation of the healing. Peter explains it to all after he enters the Temple (Acts 3:15-16). Even if one adopts Howard's interpretation mentioned above (see p. 42) that this person suffered from "hysterical paralysis" (Howard 2001: 301–05), the rite of symbolic healing is nonetheless effective, as medical anthropologists readily admit.

Recall that Strelan (2000) observed that the healing reports in Acts which use the Greek verb translated as "gaze" or "stare" or "look intently at" (e.g., Acts 3:4) very often indicates that the healer is in trance (see p. 40 above). Thus, trance is often a component part of the healing rite. The subject of this Greek verb is a holy person, and God customarily communicates with human beings in altered states of consciousness (1 Sam 3:1). One of the chief tasks of a holy person is to mediate healing from the realm of God to sick people. The person is often at prayer in connection with the healing rite. Finally, gazing, staring, or looking intently is not only a sign of being in trance but also a strategy or part of another rite for inducing trance.

What might a ceremony for inducing trance look like? Because trance is basically a neuro-physiological event, it is fitting to begin with that information. Trance can be induced "from the bottom up" or "from the top down" (d'Aquili and Newberg 2000: 91–93). Inducing a trance "from the bottom up" primarily involves the autonomic nervous system (and the brain). The two parts of the autonomic nervous system are the sympathetic nervous system (the arousal system, "fight or flight") and the parasympathetic nervous system (the quiescent system, the one that maintains homeostasis). By stimulating the senses (arousal) through rhythmic hand-clapping, drumming, shaking a rattle, or something similar, one can induce a brief but intense trance. The same can be achieved by quieting the senses (turning off all music, shutting out all noise, relaxing, etc.).

Inducing a trance "from the top down" primarily involves the brain (and the nervous system). Meditation or intense concentration is a major strategy for inducing this kind of trance. In this process, the trance begins in the cortex of the brain and then moves down into the autonomic nervous system. The positive form of meditation or concentration is to focus on one idea to the exclusion of everything else. St. Francis of Assisi often went into trance by meditating on the Passion of Jesus (Bonaventure, *Major Life* XIII). The negative form of meditation consists in striving to clear all ideas from one's mind. Both strategies (from the bottom up and from the top down) can induce an altered state of consciousness, a different level of awareness.

As already noted, d'Aquili and Newberg (2001: 104–7) describe the Roman Catholic liturgy as a mainly "slow rite," which is most likely to induce a trance "from the bottom up." This is so because of the many rhythmic components in liturgy: songs, hymns, chants, refrains, prayers, and "marked" rite gestures such as bows, genuflections, prostrations, crossing oneself, extending the arms in prayer, the use of incense, and the like. Such actions draw attention to themselves as different from ordinary baseline behaviors and stimulate a sense of awe or, in biblical language, "fear of the Lord."

The original architects of the Roman liturgy seem to have intended the worship service to serve this purpose, namely, to guide the worshipers into trance so as to encounter God. The ceremonial texts makes that clear. Among the prayers exchanged by the celebrant and the congregation after the Offertory, at the beginning of the Preface is the exhortation: "Lift up your hearts." This may be a second-century mantra for inducing trance. The response: "We have lifted them up to the Lord" is the congregation's reply: we are already in trance, we are already in the realm of God (alternate reality). Each preface of every liturgy concludes with familiar verses that allude to the vision or altered state of consciousness in which Isaiah was called to be a prophet (Isa 6:3): "Holy, holy, holy Lord God of hosts. Heaven and earth are filled with your glory." The worshipers have ascended to the Throne of God in order to join the angelic choir which sings this unending hymn to God. The rhythmicity of the liturgy can induce a trance in which to travel to the realm of God in order to encounter the deity at the Throne.

This understanding is quite explicit in the second century *The Apocryphal Letter of James*. (This James is the brother of Jesus, and this document from Egypt attests to the primacy of James over Peter and is a source and witness to the Jesus tradition known as "Jewish Christianity.") According to this letter, Jesus manifested himself for the last time to his brother James and the fisherman Peter on Ascension Day before he ascended to the sky.

> After He [Jesus] had said this, He departed.
> But we knelt down, I [James] and Peter
> *We gave thanks* and *sent* up our *hearts* toward the heavens.
> We heard with our ears and saw with our eyes
> the sound of wars and a trumpet sound and a great
>   disturbance.
> And when we had passed beyond that place,
> we sent up our minds still higher
> and we saw with our eyes and heard with our ears
> hymns and praises of the angels and a rejoicing of angels
> and greatnesses of the heavens were singing hymns
> *and we also were rejoicing.* (Nag Hammadi Codex I.15.5-23;
>   Quispel's translation, p. 71; the words in italics resonate
>   with the responses in the Roman liturgy)

James and Peter went to the first heaven of the seven planets where a war raged between good and evil spirits. Then they went still higher to the second heaven of fixed stars where angels sing hymns of praise to honor God. Notice that James and Peter are in the sky, and they join in the songs of the angels. As

Goodman has noted, one purpose of trance is to make sky journeys (Goodman 1990: 71–88; 1997; Gore 1995: 163–208) as did John, the author of Revelation (Malina and Pilch 2000).

Sky journeys were very popular in the first century A.D. and attested to in much ancient literature. Cicero (106–43 B.C.E.) recounts the "Dream of Scipio" in which a Roman general looks down from the Milky Way upon the rest of the universe (Cicero, *The Republic* VI: 9–26). He learns that all souls come here but only those who devoted themselves to the honor of their country reach the gates of heaven. Then Scipio learns his destiny, which anthropologists know is one of the major purposes of the altered states of consciousness experiences recorded in ethnographies.

The so-called Mithras Liturgy (around the second century A.D., very popular with the Roman officer corps) used "astrology and magic to provide a liturgical spell for the ecstatic ascent of the soul to God" (Meyer 1987: 211). Here the visitor gained divine revelation and immortalization. Among the Dead Sea Scrolls, *The Songs of the Sabbath Sacrifice,* composed and used by the Qumran Community, directed its members as a community to experience being in the heavenly sanctuary with the angels who sing praises to God. This communal experience quite likely occurred in group-type trance, examples of which we have seen in Acts (glossolalia; the baptism of Cornelius' household).

The Hermetic Gnostics, a secret society in Alexandria, Egypt, had rites that included the kiss of peace, baptism, or rebirth in the Spirit, and a sacred meal of the members. The aim of these Gnostics was to eventually work their way to a realm beyond the seven planets to see God. "And then stripped of the effects of the cosmic framework, the Gnostic enters the region of the Ogdoad: he becomes his real Self and with the celestial beings on high he hymns the Father (*Poimandres* 26). This, of course, happened at death, but during life it was possible to take a journey to the sky: "You heavenly Powers all, sing the hymn with me" (*Corpus Hermeticum* XIII.18).

One of the earlier resonances with the "holy, holy, holy" of the Catholic liturgy is this statement by Clement of Rome writing to believers in Corinth (A.D. 95–96):

> Let us consider the vast multitude of His angels, and see how they stand in readiness to minister to His will. For the Scripture says: "Ten thousand thousand stood ready before Him, and a thousand thousand minister to Him [Dan 7:10], and cried out: Holy, Holy, Holy is the Lord of Hosts; the whole creation is replete with His splendor." And so we, too, being dutifully assembled with one accord, should as with one voice, cry out to Him earnestly, so that we may participate in His great and glorious promises" (1 Clement 34:4-7).

Though Quispel believes that this is the oldest testimony of the Roman Mass (1998: 76), Jungman hesitated to draw that conclusion (Jungmann 1955: 132). Nevertheless, both agree that this prayer ("holy, holy, holy") was used by believers from the earliest times. Quispel's major contribution was to point out that this prayer certainly signaled that the worshipers were in an altered state of consciousness and even making sky journeys to the realm of God to sing songs of praise with the angels.

In 1979, a colleague at Georgetown University, G. Ronald Murphy, S.J., analyzed the entire Mass from the perspective of cognitive neuroscience being developed at that time by Eugene d'Aquili (Murphy 1979: 318–41). Beginning with the entrance rite and ending with the dismissal, he identified the elements of the liturgy that contributed to inducing altered states of consciousness. At the beginning of the rite, the entrance of the celebrant and ministers grabs the focus of the distracted congregation. This is called "entrainment." The ceremony creates a feeling of unity in the group. Communal recitation or singing of the "Glory to God" offers the opportunity for rite identification with the angelic choir both in Bethlehem and in the realm of God, also an opportunity for a brief trance experience.

The ceremony of alternating prayers between celebrant and congregants occasions synchronization of affect and enhances communal entrainment already begun. The service of the word brings to mind for the worshipers the latent discourse of the tradition which will assist in interpreting a trance experience if and when it takes place. In the prayers that then follow (Offertory, Preface, Consecration), the celebrant's role is to continue to synchronize the prayers of all and to facilitate trance by announcing the texts and executing "marked gestures" in a way that can contribute to trance.

The Communion ceremony crowns the unitive experience of the congregation. Sharing a sign or gesture of peace with the words of the risen Jesus: "Peace be with you" (John 20: 19, 21, 26) puts the congregation once more into the realm of God with Jesus, our ancestors, our departed loved ones. The risen Jesus surprised his disciples when he appeared to them, but modern believers ought not be surprised. For two thousand years, believers have encountered Jesus and God in altered states of consciousness experiences, and the liturgy is a privileged opportunity for this encounter. The challenge offered by this part of the ceremony is that believers should strive to deepen their union with the risen Jesus and through him reach greater intimacy with God. Murphy calls this a ceremony "of heavenly friendship and greeting."

What more remains to be said? The Roman rite is very brief after Communion. The worshipers are now in full communion with the Father, their relationship and communion with God strengthened, so a brief prayer is followed by the dismissal.

As d'Aquili and Newberg observe, a liturgy that integrates elements of arousal and of quiescence—some up-tempo songs, some slow hymns; some words of love alternating with words of fear, etc.—will help worshipers experience many aspects of God. In fact, if the rhythmicity is exceptionally effective, they may experience close unity with the other worshipers, and even feel more intensely united to God and God's companions in the divine realm.

Appendix 3

A Ceremonial Rite for Experiencing the Realm of God in Altered States of Consciousness

Stan Krippner (1972: 1–5) has enumerated twenty different states of consciousness: dreaming, sleeping, hypnagogic (drowsiness before sleep), hypnopompic (semi-consciousness preceding waking), hyperalert, lethargic, rapture, hysteric, fragmentation, regressive, meditative, trance, reverie, daydreaming, internal scanning, stupor, coma, stored memory, expanded consciousness, and "normal." These states of consciousness actually shade one into another along a continuum with "alert" at one end and deep states (trance) at the other. Human beings shift levels of consciousness many times during the day, often without realizing the shift has taken place. These can be termed spontaneous trance experiences.

It is also possible to intentionally induce trance experiences. Common strategies include listening to music, viewing art, drinking alcohol, and the like. Dr. Felicitas Goodman, however, has long been interested in ecstatic trance, especially since learning from her own research and that of Dr. Erika Bourguignon that trance states were not only normal but institutionalized into religious practices of ninety-six percent of the 486 small societies that they studied in the database of the Human Relations Area Files at Yale University (Gore 1995: 4). Dr. Goodman also recognized that ancient rites might serve as models for contemporary human beings, but they were embedded in a social context that could not be duplicated. Eventually, she formulated and teaches a ceremonial rite in The Cuyamungue Institute that accords with ethnographic evidence and contemporary insights from neuroscience. She also added native American, that is, hunter-gatherer, cultural elements to the rite (Goodman 1990: 8–26; Gore 1995: 31–40). I have modified this ceremonial rite in seeking to imitate our ancestors in faith as reflected in the Bible but especially Acts of the Apostles, using Dr. Goodman's model as a heuristic tool.

In Table 1 below, I list fourteen episodes in which persons experience a change in level of awareness during which they communicate with God or the realm of God.

Spontaneous trances	Acts 5:19; 12:6-11: Peter escapes prison
	Acts 8:26-40: An angel directs Philip
	Acts 9:10-16: Ananias learns about Paul
	Acts 11:28: Agabus predicts a famine
	Acts 16:6-8: Spirit thwarts the travel plans of Paul and Silas
	Acts 16:9-10: Paul is directed to Macedonia
	Acts 18:9-10: Ephesians speak in tongues and prophecy
	Acts 19:13-16: Evil spirits overpower sons of Sceva
	Acts 20:22-24: Spirit warns Paul
	Acts 21:4: Spirit advises Paul against going to Jerusalem
	Acts 21:9: Philip's daughters prophesy
	Acts 21:10-11: Agabus performs prophetic symbolic action on Paul
	Acts 23:11: Lord tells Paul to bear witness in Rome
	Acts 27:23-24: Guardian angel assures Paul of safe arrival in Rome

Table 1: Spontaneous Trance Experiences in Acts

In Table 2 below, I present some basic elements of a ceremonial rite for intentionally inducing a trance patterned after that of Dr. Goodman. Information about spontaneous and intentionally induced trance experiences (e.g., healing trances) reported in Acts of the Apostles would seem to confirm the validity of the proposed rite.

Intentionally induced trances	
1. Fasting (sensory deprivation)	Acts 9:9-12: Paul was fasting for three days when he had a vision of Ananias restoring his sight Acts 10:10: Peter was hungry at noon when he fell into trance Acts 13:1-3: Prophets and teachers in the church in Antioch were praying and fasting when they received instruction from the Spirit
2. Selecting an **appropriate place**; a "sacred" space with "sacred" objects	Acts 2:1-4: Spirit descends on the group gathered together and inspires glossolalia Acts 22:17-18: The Lord warned Paul at prayer in the Temple to flee Jerusalem
3. Deciding on the **technique** for visiting the realm of God: a ritual posture, or reading from Scripture or another part of the tradition; use of incense or candles; prayer, meditation; story telling; or a combination of techniques.	Acts 1:14; 2:1: The group was at prayer when the Spirit descended Acts 3:4: Peter "stared" at the lame man to induce a healing trance Acts 6:17–7:60: Stephen's speech (storytelling) induced his trance and/or enhanced it

Table 2: A Ceremonial Rite for Intentionally Induced Trances Based on Acts

Table 2 (cont'd)

3. (The sense of smell is known by neurologists as an ergotropic driver, that is, an element that stimulates the arousal system and leads to trance [d'Aquili and Newberg 1993: 31], hence the value of burning incense.)	Acts 9:11: Paul was fasting and praying when he received a follow-up vision to his call vision Acts 10:9-23; 11:1-14: Peter was at prayer [and hungry] when he had his vision of animals on the sheet Acts 10:44-49; 11:15-18: Peter's speech to Cornelius' household induced the trance state in which the Spirit descended on them and inspired glossolalia Acts 22:17: Paul at prayer in the Temple is advised by the Lord to flee Jerusalem
4. **Preparing oneself/one's body** for encountering beings from the realm of God (purification rite): incense and prayer can be used as purifying agents, among other elements.	Acts 5:19: Peter was prepared for the visit of the angel who liberated him from prison Acts 6:15: Stephen's face resembling "the face of an angel" indicates he was prepared and perhaps already in trance Acts 8:26-40: Philip was prepared to communicate with an angel Acts 10:3-6, 30-32: Cornelius was at prayer when the angel visited him
5. **Preparing the mind** Breathing is an easy and popular strategy to quiet the mind. Concentrate on the process of taking fifty slow, deep breaths (inhalation, exhalation, and pause constitutes one breath).	No specific mention of such an "exercise," though a number of trance experiences took place in prayer (see #3 above)

Table 2 (cont'd)

6a. A **trance "from bottom up"** requires sensory (over) stimulation: for example, the sound of rhythmic rattling, or drumming, about 200 to 210 beats a minute for 15 minutes, the optimal period of time. Any source of rhythmicity including patterned behavior itself (as in the liturgy, see Appendix 2, p. 179) is ideally suited for inducing a trance "from the bottom up."	Acts 13:9-12: By "looking intently" at Bar-Jesus (sensory overstimulation), Paul enters trance and declares that God will blind the magician Acts 14:8-10: Looking intently at a man lame from birth, Paul entered a healing trance
6b. A **trance "from top down"** can occur in two ways: in the positive mode: one concentrates on one idea to the exclusion of others (the Passion of Jesus), or an image from scripture (e.g., the bent woman, Luke 13:10-17); or listen intently to music such as a Taizé refrain (e.g., *Ubi Caritas);* in the negative mode, one strives to clear the mind of all thoughts.	Acts 9:3-6; 22:4-11; 26:9-18: Paul's intense mental concentration on members of the Jesus group whom he was persecuting triggered his encounter with the risen Jesus in trance Acts 10:19 Pondering the meaning of his first vision (Acts 10:10-16), Peter receives instruction from the Spirit in trance
7. **Record and interpret the trance** (see Jer 30:2; 36:2; Hab 2:2). In a group experience, share and discuss. The group experience is especially helpful in the interpretation.	The speeches of Peter interpret trance experiences (Acts 2:14-41; 3:12-26; 10:34-43) just as Paul interprets his (Acts 9:3-6; 22:4-11; 26:9-18)

There are three stages to a typical trance experience, though they need not be present in every trance. Here in brief are the stages.

Stage 1	geometric patterns; light (white) color
Stage 2	imposing meaning on the patterns
Stage 3	deepest stage; subject enters into the scenes and becomes part of the imagery.

Table 3: The Stages of Trance

In stage 1, the lightest stage, one sees geometric patterns or figures like dots, lattice work, grids, zig-zag lines. These flicker, scintillate, expand, contract, and combine with one another, but are independent of an external source of light. The prevalent color is white. The bright light in Paul's call-visions indicates Stage 1 of trance (Acts 9:3-6; 22:4-11; 26:9-18). The trance ritual is customarily performed with eyes closed, so the colors are not reflecting external sight. In Stage 2, the subject tries to make sense of these geometric forms by seeing them as objects or experiences familiar or important to her or him. The person draws on culture's latent discourse, or a sacred tradition, or some other source of meaning to begin interpreting what is being seen. (In Paul's call vision, he heard a voice, asked who was speaking, and when he learned the identity, began to make sense of what he was experiencing. He has erred in persecuting members of the Jesus group because he has misunderstood Jesus. Acts 9 and parallels.) Finally, in stage 3, the deepest stage of trance, the subject might enter into the scene and become part of the imagery rather than just an observer. Peter's escapes from prison probably took place in the deepest stages of a trance whence his puzzlement about whether it was really happening or only a "vision" (Acts 5:19; 12:6-11). Sometimes people undergo frightening or exhilarating transformations (metamorphoses). When Stephen's face is perceived to resemble "the face of an angel," it probably indicates that he is in a deep stage of trance (Acts 6:15). At other times, there are no images, and the experience is more visceral or kinesthetic than visual.

This is a project in progress with assistance from members of The Cuyamungue Institute. Readers interested in contributing suggestions for the proposed rite or sharing experiences are invited to do so. Here are some relevant web-sites and contacts:

pilchj@georgetown.edu

My web page: http: //www.georgetown.edu/faculty/pilchj

The Cuyamungue Institute:
http: //www.ritualbodypostures.com/

Index of Authors

Index of Scripture

Index of Subjects